THE NEW LAKE POETS

The New Lake Poets

EDITED BY
WILLIAM SCAMMELL

BLOODAXE BOOKS

ISBN: 1 85224 146 2

First published 1991 by
Bloodaxe Books Ltd,
P.O. Box 1SN,
Newcastle upon Tyne NE99 1SN.

Bloodaxe Books Ltd acknowledges
the financial assistance of Northern Arts.

ACKNOWLEDGEMENTS

Thanks are due to Drs A. & A. Dalzell,
owners of the cover painting by Anna Fell, and to
the South Bank Centre's Exhibitions Department,
for their assistance; and to Sheila Fell
for giving her permission for it to be used
on this book.

Cover reproduction by V & H Reprographics, Newcastle upon Tyne.

Typesetting by Bryan Williamson, Darwen, Lancashire.

Printed in Great Britain by
Bell & Bain Limited, Glasgow, Scotland.

Contents

Introduction

There was only ever one Lake Poet, and that was Wordsworth. He knew Cumbria, its landscape and its people, as closely as he knew his own heartbeat, fusing inner and outer together in a poetry of colossal penetration and calm. Coleridge produced one masterpiece while he lived at Keswick, the verse letter to Sara Hutchinson which later became the *Dejection Ode*, but he stayed only three years, on and off, and his gift was already on the verge of dissipation. Though he delighted at first in the mountains and incomparable vistas from his study window ('the best view in England') his genius was fully formed before he took up residence here; and there is evidence that he found the 'smothering weight' and sombre self-sufficiency of the fells as much a threat as an inspiration – 'I may not hope from outward forms to win/ The passion and the life whose fountains are within.' Southey settled in Greta Hall for the duration (forty years, to be precise) and so became a local by adoption, but lives more vividly in Byron's satires, and in various memoirs, than in his own verse.

Shelley passed through, and so, more briefly, did Keats, simply because of Wordsworth's presence. Other temporary residents include De Quincey, a real writer but not a poet; 'Christopher North' (the pen-name of John Wilson), whose life is more interesting than his work; and Coleridge's eldest son Hartley, known affectionately to the locals as 'laal 'Artley', who was on better terms with the Grasmere pubs than with the muse. Later still Tennyson was a regular visitor at Mirehouse on the shores of Bassenthwaite; Doctor Arnold introduced the young Matthew to the area; Ruskin settled at Coniston; and even Hopkins came on a day-trip to see his friend Canon Dixon at Hayton, Carlisle. None of these, however, owed anything essential to Cumbria.

The next approximation to a Lake Poet, it might be argued, was the young Auden, who spent many summers at his father's holiday home in Wescoe, near Threlkeld, and made good if oblique use of 'the stone smile of this country god' in his early verse. With Norman Nicholson (1914-1987), Cumbrian born and bred, the wheel comes full circle. Norman, whom several of us in this anthology knew, might be regarded as one of the tutelary spirits of the area, so it is fitting that his fine poem on Wordsworth should stand at the gateway to this collection of new Cumbrian poetry. I am grateful to Elizabeth Joyce for permission to print his last published poem 'Epithalamium for a Niece', and to Peggy Troll for the previously-unpublished 'Comet Come'.

The writers gathered together here share a commitment to poetry and loyalty to an area which has shown itself friendly to the meditative, individual voice. As in the case of the original Lake School, they are nearly all "offcomers". (The three exceptions are Peter Rafferty, Mick North and Ben Scammell.) Geoffrey Holloway settled in Staveley, near Kendal, in 1953, where he lives with his wife Patricia Pogson; Elizabeth Delmore at Bassenthwaite in 1964; Neil Curry in Ulverston in 1974; Christopher Pilling (who was evacuated to Cumbria as a child) in Keswick in 1978; David Scott, vicar of a country parish, at Torpenhow, near Ireby, in 1980; David Lindley in Cockermouth in 1980; David Morley in Bowness in 1985; Meg Peacocke at a lonely hill-farm on Stainmore in 1987. I moved to Cockermouth in 1975, and for twelve years we have run an informal poetry workshop which meets once a month to discuss new work and provide a sympathetic but critical forum for the airing of syllables and souls. Annie Foster, Peter Rafferty and Charles McDonald all live in Carlisle, where I run another workshop under the auspices of the Continuing Education department of Newcastle University. Maggie Hannan moved to Garrigill, near Alston, in 1985. David Wright lived at Braithwaite, near Keswick, for many years, then moved to Appleby-in-Westmorland.

There is plenty to admire and to enjoy in the work of these poets, who are as diverse as they are scrupulous to their own perception of things. Christopher Pilling writes a witty, formalist poetry which nods in the direction of Wallace Stevens's 'supreme fiction' (i.e. the workings of the imagination) but which never slights emotion in favour of aestheticism. Recurring themes include painting (especially Matisse), music, insects, and domestic love. He handles the imagination with a down-to-earth tact, and conversely subjects the mundane to a quizzical sense of wonder. David Scott stands in the long line of country poet-priests, from George Herbert to R.S. Thomas; and owes something also to the tradition represented by Hardy and Edward Thomas. His quiet, understated verse is as exact as the bolts on the gate of the auctioneer's ring in 'Kirkwall Auction Mart', and yet can unexpectedly soar too, like the 'wreath of snorted breath' from the frightened cattle in the same poem, going up to heaven like a prayer. His poems keep a knowledgeable eye on this world as well as the next, trying to give both their due. The result is a highly Anglican fusion of prayer and practicality, a manual of attitudes validated by daily use rather than by revelation. Neil Curry shares something of Pilling's interest in the American moderns, mediated perhaps in his case by the influenceof Charles Tomlinson, his tutor at university. Curry seldom uses metre or rhyme, however, preferring free verse or syllabics in order to preserve a contemporary tone of voice, one which ranges freely over natural and cultural history, seeking to place the self unselfconsciously in the rich context of English humanism, whether religious, scientific, or poetic.

Geoffrey Holloway is, with David Wright, one of the older and more established figures in this collection. He served as a paratrooper in the Second World War with a field ambulance corps, an experience finely commemorated in his book *Rhine Jump*, and has published widely in all the poetry magazines over the past thirty years. His long service as a social worker has also contributed to the fierce honesty of his eye. Patricia Pogson's virtues are founded on brevity and emotional tact, whether focussed on a natural history which reflects our own ('Bee', 'Exits') or on the fragile egos observed and explored in such poems as 'Face Mask' and 'Hairdressing'. Annie Foster shares these qualities, together with a toughly ironic awareness of the disparity between life as it ought ideally to be and life as it is actually lived ('Starting School', 'No Dice', 'Caterpillar'). Her directness, and the organisation of her material, may owe something to the example of David Scott, but the sensibility winning its way through to a qualified joy is uniquely her own.

David Morley read Biology at Bristol University where, like Curry and Ben Scammell, he received warm encouragement from Charles Tomlinson. Tomlinson has said that perception enforces its own morality; clear seeing is a precondition of clear thinking. Conversely, sloppy or inchoate ways of seeing imply sloppy habits of mind, and thus a dubious morality. Morley's responses to the natural world parallel his excited responses to art. Mick North's poetry shows traces of an engagement with Ted Hughes's, and also with Tony Harrison's. His rural England is one given over to pieties hard-won from a life of physical toil and few amenities. It's good to see him exploiting and refining traditional metres and rhymes, or half-rhymes, in order to express thoroughly contemporary emotions. Maggie Hannan's muse turns her face away from comfortable orthodoxies to confront loneliness and hurt, and the energies generated in surviving them. I enjoy the packed, physical nature of the movement of her lines. Meg Peacocke's poems are recognisably in the tradition fostered by Larkin, which juxtaposes the wry and the everyday with long perspectives. She has the true poet's obsession with words, and cadences, and things, and the infinity of roots that lie tangled beneath them.

Like Morley, Peter Rafferty trained as a scientist, a fact visible in his learned geological references and minute interest in the weathering of rock. He has an engaging throwaway manner, liking to confide his subject-matter in long digressive sentences, and is also an excellent translator, as the examples included here demonstrate. Charles McDonald is more likely to tackle things head-on, 'pinpointing odd images' in search of 'Body/ And soul' ('At the Gwen John Exhibition'). 'Asdrubal Jiménez' shows what can still be done with a poetry of direct statement, content simply to record the facts. Elizabeth Delmore and David Lindley write a lucid, traditional poetry, responding very directly to people and places. Ben Scammell, on the other hand, the youngest contributor represented, has a dry, oblique slant on Cumbria and on the media-soaked tides of contemporary fashion, and clearly owes something to the Modernists and their successors. David Wright is too well-known to need any introduction here.

None of these poets belongs to any particular school, nor do they wave any flags of allegiance, except to human feeling and discrimination. I hope you enjoy their work as much as I do.

WILLIAM SCAMMELL
Cockermouth, Cumbria

Publisher's Note: William Scammell did not include any of his own work in this anthology, but at our request he has allowed us to print a selection of his poems.

Norman Nicholson

MATT SIMPSON

NORMAN NICHOLSON (1914-1987) was born in
Millom, Cumbria, where he lived all his life.
He was the author of six books of poems (most
recently *Selected Poems 1940-1982* [Faber,
1982]), four verse plays, two novels, numer-
ous books and anthologies about the Lake
District, and the autobiography *Wednesday
Early Closing* (Faber, 1975). He received the
Queen's Gold Medal for Poetry in 1977. ●

ACKNOWLEDGEMENTS: Norman
Nicholson: *Selected Poems 1940-
1982* (Faber, 1982); *Between
Comets*, ed. William Scammell
(Taxus, 1984), poems reproduced
by permission of David Higham
Associates Ltd.

To the River Duddon

I wonder, Duddon, if you still remember
An oldish man with a nose like a pony's nose,
Broad bones, legs long and lean but strong enough
To carry him over Hard Knott at seventy years of age.
He came to you first as a boy with a fishing-rod
And a hunk of Anne Tyson's bread and cheese in his pocket,
Walking from Hawkshead across Walna Scar;
Then as a middle-aged Rydal landlord,
With a doting sister and a government sinecure,
Who left his verses gummed to your rocks like lichen,
The dry and yellow edges of a once-green spring.
He made a guide-book for you, from your source
There where you bubble through the moss on Wrynose
(Among the ribs of bald and bony fells
With screes scratched in the turf like grey scabs),
And twist and slither under humpbacked bridges –
Built like a child's house from odds and ends
Of stones that lie about the mountain side –
Past Cockley Beck Farm and on to Birk's Bridge,
Where the rocks stride about like legs in armour,
And the steel birches buckle and bounce in the wind
With a crinkle of silver foil in the crisp of the leaves;

On then to Seathwaite, where like a steam-navvy
You shovel and slash your way through the gorge
By Wallabarrow Crag, broader now
From becks that flow out of black upland tarns
Or ooze through golden saxifrage and the roots of rowans;
Next Ulpha, where a stone dropped from the bridge
Swims like a tadpole down thirty feet of water
Between steep skirting-boards of rock; and thence
You dribble into lower Dunnerdale
Through wet woods and wood-soil and woodland flowers,
Tutson, the St John's-wort with a single yellow bead,
Marsh marigold, creeping jenny and daffodils;
Here from hazel islands in the late spring
The catkins fall and ride along the stream
Like little yellow weasels, and the soil is loosed
From bulbs of the white lily that smells of garlic,
And dippers rock up and down on rubber legs,
And long-tailed tits are flung through the air like darts;
By Foxfield now you taste the salt in your mouth,
And thrift mingles with the turf, and the heron stands
Watching the wagtails. Wordsworth wrote:
'Remote from every taint of sordid industry.'
But you and I know better, Duddon.
For I, who've lived for nearly thirty years
Upon your shore, have seen the slagbanks slant
Like screes into the sand, and watched the tide
Purple with ore back up the muddy gullies,
And wiped the sinter dust from the farmyard damsons.
A hundred years of floods and rain and wind
Have washed your rocks clear of his words again,
Many of them half-forgotten, brimming the Irish Sea,
But that which Wordsworth knew, even the old man
When poetry had failed like desire, was something
I have yet to learn, and you, Duddon,
Have learned and re-learned to forget and forget again.
Not the radical, the poet and heretic,
To whom the water-forces shouted and the fells
Were like a blackboard for the scrawls of God,
But the old man, inarticulate and humble,
Knew that eternity flows in a mountain beck –
The long cord of the water, the shepherd's numerals
That run upstream, through the singing decades of dialect.

He knew, beneath mutation of year and season,
Flood and drought, frost and fire and thunder,
The blossom on the rowan and the reddening of the berries,
There stands the base and root of the living rock,
Thirty thousand feet of solid Cumberland.

From a Boat at Coniston

I look into the lake (the lacquered water
Black with the sunset), watching my own face.
Tiny red-ribbed fishes swim
In and out of the nostrils, long-tongued weeds
Lick at the light that oozes down from the surface,
And bubbles rise from the eyes like aerated
Tears shed there in the element of mirrors.
My sight lengthens its focus; sees the sky
Laid level upon the glass, the loud
World of the wind and the map-making clouds and history
Squinting over the rim of the fell. The wind
Lets on the water, paddling like a duck,
And face and cloud are grimaced out
In inch-deep wrinkles of the moving waves.
A blackbird clatters; alder leaves
Make mooring buoys for the water beetles.
I wait for the wind to drop, against hope
Hoping, and against the weather, yet to see
The water empty, the water full of itself,
Free of the sky and the cloud and free of me.

Epithalamium for a Niece

'Who gives this woman to this man?'
The parson asks, and one man can,
According to the liturgy,
Rightly reply. And many more,
If saying 'I do' were the door

To show their daughters out, would say
It now and twenty times a day.
But with 'I do' or merely 'Me',
Failing the Prayer Book's nudge, who'd claim
Just cause or just justification
To dare the pride of giving? Let
Church and choir and congregation
Silent remain and the reply
Come from some other than the 'I'
That hesitates at 'Do'. The wind
Might say: 'I gave her breath'; the sky:
'I gave the light to see her by';
Soil and humus, stem and stone:
'We gave the calcium for the bone,
Carbohydrates, minerals, those
Hormones and genes and chromosomes
That chose her sex and shaped her nose.'
Water might lap and lip: 'From me
Venus was born, so why not she?'
But neither earth nor sky nor water
Speak sponsorship for this their daughter.
So in the eternity before
'I do' is done, and while the air
Waits on the Prayer Book's questionnaire,
Let silence ring its loud reply;
'She gives herself – what can a man ask more?'

Five Minutes

'I'm having five minutes,' he said,
Fitting the shelter of the cobble wall
Over his shoulders like a cape. His head
Was wrapped in a cap as green
As the lichened stone he sat on. The winter wind
Whined in the ashes like a saw,
And thorn and briar shook their red
Badges of hip and haw;
The fields were white with smoke of blowing lime;
Rusty iron brackets of sorrel stood

In grass grey as the whiskers round an old dog's nose.
'Just five minutes,' he said;
And the next day I heard that he was dead,
Having five minutes to the end of time.

Comet Come
(for Peggy)

It's here at last. Eyes in the know
Had spotted it two years ago,
A microscopic smut on film.
The probes are launched; binoculars
Lurk ready on dark attic stairs,
Waiting and hoping. But for what?
For Giotto's Star of Bethlehem,
Or that bright threatener in the sky
That twanged a spike through Harold's eye
And dumped a Norman on the throne?
Those nightly-watched incendiary flashes
That put a match to London town
And burnt the stews and steeples down,
Searing the Plague among their ashes,
Or, in black, after-chapel air,
The admonitory naphtha-flare
Our fathers saw, whose motto read:
'War coming and King Edward dead.'

Prompt as an actor to his cue,
It teeters feebly into view,
A dirty snowball, chimney-high,
Faint phosphorescence in the sky,
Not up to candle-power – a barely
Distinguishable blur, as if
God in an artist's dab and doubt
Had sketched a star and thumbed it out.
We search and strain – but with a hiss
The clouds swish over like a curtain,
Blacking the scene out, and, uncertain
Which smudge is which, we rub sore eyes,

Wondering why on earth we've waited
Seventy years and more for this.
Where is the pride of mathematics
When magi and magicians (no
Newton or Einstein in their credo)
Can manage to see more than we do?

Anxious astronomers protest:
Give them a month, they'll know just what
The frozen core is made of, test
The fluorescence tailing from it,
Fanned out in the solar wind,
Promising faithfully the comet
Will shine as it has never shone
In Twenty Hundred and Sixty-One.
(By which time they'll contrive together
Even to guarantee the weather.)

But in that year of Sixty-One
What will the comet look down on?
A wiser world, or one unpeopled,
Dead as the asteroidal dust
It hoovers, on its orbit, through?
Will telescopes still sweep the view
With no-one to stare up them? Must
Satellites circle aimlessly
A circling satellite? Or when
Halley returns next time but ten
Will toe- and finger-counting men,
On unpolluted islands, pray,
In awe and wonder once again:
'Thy comet come, O Lord, Amen.'

Neil Curry

NEIL CURRY was born in Newcastle in 1937.
He has lectured in English at the University
of Guelph, Canada, and taught at Oundle
School. His verse translations of Euripides
have been published by Doubleday, Meth-
uen, and Cambridge University Press. He is
the author of *Ships in Bottles* (Enitharmon
Press 1988), a Poetry Book Society Recom-
mendation. ●

ACKNOWLEDGEMENTS: Neil Curry:
Ships in Bottles (Enitharmon,
1988); *The Orange Dove of Fiji*,
ed. Simon Rae (Hutchinson,
1989).

In a Calendar of Saints

I

Wondering which of all the saints
Had been assigned to share the hours with me
On this first day of February,
(The snow beginning to thaw outside
As though touched by these jets of flame-blue
Hyacinth burning in the window)
I found not one name but two: Ignatius
Of Antioch, and Saint Brigid.

Arrested, and shipped in fetters
Back to Trajan's Rome, Ignatius,
Intent upon martyrdom, begged
That no one intercede for him. 'I am
God's own grain,' he wrote, pausing
Among his strictures on the Trinity
And Eucharist, 'and will prove good bread
Though ground in the jaws of the arena's beasts.'

But in Kildare there was no lion's tooth,
Just the dandelion: Brigid's flower.
Patron of things new-born, who turned water
Into milk, not wine, hers is the other
Face of the world. And on Candlemas Eve
She comes to us with her lambs, quickening
The year: abbess and triple-goddess;
Bride The Beautiful: the Celtic Muse.

II

With Concordius their first foot, the saints
Go marching through the pages of the year:
Hermits, and founders of great orders,
Contemplatives, and martyrs to the Faith:
Men like Aquinas, most learned of saints
And most saintly of all the learned;
Or that other Thomas, whose turbulent brain
One Richard le Breton splattered
Over the altar-cloth at Canterbury.

Some, looking for nothing from this world,
Were, like Cuthbert, content that it should shrink
To a rock off Lindisfarne, where grey seals
Bobbed up and blinked their nostrils in surprise;
While in Assisi, Francis could not embrace
Or bless enough of it, were it his Lady
Poverty or the leper's hand. Almost blind,
In the Convent garden of San Damian
He sang his Canticle of Brother Sun:

A chorus of witness in which we hear
Pointers to what may, impossibly,
Prove possible: as when in August 1941,
On the Eve of the Feast of the Assumption,
Maximilian Kolbe, Polish priest,
In the starved dark of Cell Block 13
Took upon himself another man's death;
The carbolic acid sluiced through his veins
Winning one more victory for Golgotha.

St Kilda

I

The map the dominie had tacked up
On the schoolroom wall didn't even show
St Kilda, but then only a foreigner
Would have needed one to find his way past Mull
And Skye, out through the Sound of Harris, then on
For fifty empty miles over the
Oily pitch and swell of the grey
North Atlantic.

                    Any St Kildans,
Out of sight of land, with bad weather closing,
Knew they'd only to watch the flight-paths
Of the birds: guillemot and gannet would wreck them
On the stacs round Borreray, while puffins
Scuttering back wave-high to Dun
Would prove a safe guide home to Hirta
And the Village Bay.

II

Birds. Or angels even
They must have seemed, the women
Plucking, in a cloud of feathers
At the haul of fulmars their menfolk

Had themselves plucked off the cliffs
Of Conachair; cragsmen spidering,
Thirty fathoms down, along ledges
Of guano, dependent on sheer faith

In their neighbours and on a horsehair rope.
Claim life those cliffs could, but always would
Sustain it while there were sea-birds
In such thousands to stew or dry;

Even a gannet's neck, turned inside out,
Made a snug boot, and oil from the fulmar
Not only fuelled their lamps, but was a panacea
For no matter what ills or ailments of the island.

III

Ultima Thule it was
Until the Victorians discovered it,
Sending in their missionaries
To pound out the parable

Of the Prodigal Son
To people who hadn't
Anywhere to stray to
And had never seen a pig.

Then steamers came, and summer visitors
With gimcrack charities and new disease,
Tipping the cragsmen with a penny each
To see them capering about on Conachair;

Pennies that the winter ferryman
Would finger from the eyelids of their dead.

IV

By lantern-light
They loaded a few more
Sticks of furniture
And the last of the sheep,
And then they drowned their dogs.

In the morning,
According to custom,
In every empty house
There was a bible left
Open at Exodus.

Poppy Heads

There is, it seems, no poppy seed so old
That given a drop of water and some warmth
It will not flower again, breaking the dream
Of its opiate sleep to send new fancies
Shimmering along the blood. After twenty
Centuries, when smart industrialists
Moved back into the silver mines at Laurium
To pocket up the banks of spoil heaps,
There was a moment's hesitation

In the dust, then wild and exotic
Poppy buds came powering up – strange sons
And daughters of blooms that Pliny must have known,
And would have seen stamped out in tesserae
Upon the Aventine, and on the portly
Bellies of black amphorae: Ceres' sign:
Shocks of sheer scarlet in a yellow heat
That twined through stooks and burned against the blue:
Manna for the mind beside the body's bread.

But then what was manna? The word was no more
Than a mute echo that tried to give
A miracle a name. All they could tell
Was that it came after the quails had flown in
With the falling of the dusk and settled
Over the Wilderness of Sin: a gift
From an otherwise indifferent night
In answer to their needs, their dream; and now
An image of the fulfilment of a dream.

For dreams are not caught in the dissonant
Thickets of language, nor strung on time's links:
They come to us with all the inseminate
Anarchy of the image, and every mote
Of the past concurrent, so wherever
A poppy head has nodded in the world
Some seed may lie waiting and from the pit of night
Will delight, bewilder or admonish us
With the ambiguous innocence that is its power.

Galapagos

With FitzRoy's twenty-two chronometers
Ticking on their shelves, Darwin, sick again,
Killed time re-reading Lyell's *Geology*,
Or *Paradise Lost* – his favourite poem.

On deck the crew were plump and happy now.
Roast armadillo and ostrich dumplings
Had brought them round Cape Horn, and the *Beagle*,
Under full sail, was tacking for the Line.

But charting that long, sheep's jaw-bone of a coast
Could not assuage the zealot in FitzRoy.
To substantiate the Flood, evidence
For Genesis: that was what he wanted.

When they landed, Antediluvium
Was at every turn, but nowhere Eden;
Not in such heat; not with such contortions
Of cinder and lava; and not with such

Black Imps of Hell as the iguanas
Crawling and slithering about these Blighted
Encantadas – these Enchanted Islands,
Where the chief sound of life was a hiss –

From the snakes, and from the giant tortoises,
The indomitable galapagos themselves,
As they lurched and lumbered their way inland
Following their ancient paths to water.

Yet in all this new weird, it was the beaks
Of brown finches that dismasted FitzRoy,
And sent him on his solitary way
To slash a red equator round his throat.

Swallows and Tortoises

It was the Age of Reason.
And when spring broke in Selborne
And Timothy the tortoise did come forth

And march about, they had a feel
For his pulse, but could not find it;
Bawled at him through a speaking trumpet,
But he appeared not to regard it;

So they dunked him in a tub of water
To see if he could swim, and watched him
Go sinking down to scrabble on the bottom,
Quite out of his element, and seemingly

Much dismayed. But what puzzled them most
In Selborne was that Providence
Should squander longevity
On a reptile who relished it so little

As to spend two-thirds of its existence
In a joyless stupor, all but the thread
Of solstitial awareness suspended.

But there were lessons to be learned everywhere,
And as Timothy awoke with the first flight
Of the swallows, might not they too
Have their hybernacula?

And had not Dr Johnson himself seen them
Conglobulate, before throwing themselves
Under water, wherein they would winter
On the bed of the river?

Sometimes Timothy escaped them,
Toddling his carapace out through the wicket:
Pursuits of an amorous kind transporting him
Beyond the bounds of his usual gravity.

Mute Swans

Why did Ben Jonson
        like a great battle fleet
Call Shakespeare
        line astern they come
A swan?
        down the river,
And of Avon too
        breaking the water
When he spent the whole of his working life
        with their silence,
By the Thames?
        and such power
He must have seen him
        in a bird,
At Stratford, I suppose,
        the great paddles of their feet
When he'd downed his quill
        working away under the surface,
And wondered at such silence
        these mute swans

Dandelion

This is time's
(one o'clock, two o'clock)
golden head
wet the bed

flower;
forever turning its
(four o'clock, five o'clock)
face

to follow the sun.
But it's time that sets the
(seven o'clock, eight o'clock)
grey hairs growing

and will scythe off its
(eleven o'clock, twelve o'clock)
limp and wrinkled
ugly bald skull.

Anne Hathaway Composes Her 18th Sonnet

I wonder what I ought to do today.
This autumn weather's still so temperate
You'd almost think that it was early Maie
And that we'd somehow muddled up the date.
I've polished all the silver till it shines;
Some bits were tarnish'd, all their sheen quite dimm'd.
I'd like some help, but Will always declines,
Says, 'Can't you see the hedge is still untrimm'd?'
I really think our love's begun to fade.
He nags me so. 'The milliner thou ow'st,'
He says, 'and did we need that new lampshade?
It's not on trees you know that money grow'st.'
        And then he's off to London with, 'I'll see
        You, chuck. Now don't you fret. I'll write to thee!'

Elizabeth Delmore

CHAPLIN'S OF KESWICK

ELIZABETH DELMORE was born in London in 1916 and brought up in north Yorkshire. After living in Canada, New Zealand, Ceylon, Austria and Switzerland, she settled in Cumbria in 1964 ('long enough in one place, at last, to put down a big tap-root'). She has written verse 'off and on' since the age of seven, and has published several pamphlets of poetry, and written a Morning Story for BBC Radio 4. ●

ACKNOWLEDGEMENTS: Elizabeth Delmore: *Rooted in Cumbria;* and Radio Carlisle.

The Difference

Touchingly alike, old man, old dog,
grizzled and battle-scarred and stiff with years
set off together for the daily walk.

Joined by the leather umbilical cord,
pace matched to pace,
patient with one another's needed pauses
they reach their goal, the known familiar bench
and rest and warm their old bones
in the pale autumn sunshine.
The old dog snaps at flies,
the old man sucks at a stumpy pipe
in silent companionship.

They saunter home
in time for Meals on Wheels.
The hurrying lady flies in with a cheerful smile:
'how are you both?' she says and dashes out
knowing full well
that the dog will get all the best bits.

Together they snooze away the afternoon.
The dog, dreaming of bones and hunts and glorious fights
and willing bitches
whimpers and twitches.
The man, dreaming of beer and hunts and glorious fights
and willing whores
mumbles and snores.

Waking, they touch each other for reassurance.
For the man, a sup of tea;
for the dog, a good worry at an old bone
and they both scratch a bit as they potter away the day
until its time for bed.

And there the likeness ends.

Blessed the dog in his animal nature:
unaware that there is a future
he can settle trustingly to sleep.

Accurst the man, endowed with power of thought:
in the weakness of age he yet must battle on
and nightly wrestle with two demon dreads.

If he this night should die,
what will become of his friend,
his old, dependent dog who needs him so?
What stranger will feed him, take him to the park
stopping at the known lamp-posts?

But there is yet a greater fear:
what if, in the night, the dog should die,
his dear, his sole companion, always there
to ward off unthinkable loneliness?

Haunted by this, the ultimate desolation,
even as he weeps
he sleeps.

Is It Not Strange?

When I recall that place
where above all other places
we were happy,
I remember clearly only two details.

In the candle-light I see
my schoolgirl watch
hung on a nail stuck into a beam.
I see the Roman figures,
the scratches on the glass,
the colour of the strap
with total clarity
although that watch was stolen
thirty years ago.

In the darkness I hear
a slithering
and a scratching
and a squeaking
as a very small mouse
climbed onto the rim of the billycan
which we had filled with water for our morning tea;
and a very small splash
as it fell in.

I got up and fished it out,
not wanting any death or bereavement
however small
to mar that place and moment.
It bit me, shook itself
and scampered off
and we laughed
and were glad.

But of all other sights and sounds
in that place
where, above all other places
we were happy,
nothing remains.

Is it not strange?

Marmalade

It snowed.

You kissed me and left and I was desolate
and in my desolation I made marmalade.
I stirred the bubbling pan as it grew dark
and was alarmed to hear footsteps.
The door flew open; there you stood, grinning;
wonderful unexpected re-assurance of love.

Spoon in hand, I ran into your arms
and the half-set brew dripped stickily
down the back of your coat.

Laughing, we disentangled ourselves;
the moment is linked forever
with the rich smell of cooking oranges.

You kissed me
and left.

I am desolate.

It is snowing.

I shall make marmalade.

It darkens as I stir the bubbling pan
remembering you standing at the door,
remembering your delight at my surprise,
remembering the texture of your coat:

remembering laughter.

The marmalade is rich; stirred memories
blend with the scent of cooking oranges
but it will have a very salty taste.

It is still snowing.

Yew

Running down the fell, I round a rock
and there you stand.
I stop for you to pass
on the narrow track;
step aside politely on the grass;
for one split second sure that it is I
who am rooted to the spot
while you
plod upward steadily towards the sky.

Willow

We are the clan of willows.
We are BAD.
We are incestuous,
promiscuous,
gregarious;
we drive poor botanists MAD.

Our elegant elderly ancestors
aloof and solitary in field and fen,
what have they to do with us
as we jostle and laugh,
stand with our feet in the mud,
crowd together by river and lake
and entangle poor fishermen?

Only garden centres
and designers of plates
make us weep.
Sometimes we keep
good company;
kingfishers perch on our branches,
otters live among our roots,
trout rest in our shadow
and to these we're a friendly tree.

If you put us on fires we spark and we spit
for our medium is water, not flame.
But remember, without us you can't make a hit
in the beautiful white English game.

Such Sweet Sorrow

The trees were hung with marzipan.

I was confused
because I don't like marzipan
but I do like trees:

So I asked my daughter for advice.
She said this confused her;
I was supposed to be the one
who gave advice
and she'd rather talk about horses.

As she spoke, horses thundered past
in a great herd, galloping East
and certainly confused
for they should have been galloping
into the sunset.

So I asked earth if she had altered direction
or if the sun was setting somewhere else
for a change. Earth said she was confused
by perpetual rotation and just wanted
to stand still for a few millennia.

I wept for earth's confusion.
Where my tears fell on the ground
trees sprang up, green and beautiful,

all hung with marzipan.

Annie Foster

ANNIE FOSTER was born in Newcastle in 1955. She trained as a teacher at Leicester College of Education, and then taught in a London comprehensive school before moving to Cumbria in 1980. She is married, and has two children. ●

SOLWAY STUDIO

The Visit

You left a message on the board
that the group should start without you.
Underneath I chalked,
'It would be like swimming without the water.'
You were savage at the apathy
and must have guessed about the love.

You kept in touch
and made one motherly trip at every new stage
then drove back to your real life.

Fifteen years on you visit
and we take one day
away from the small circle of my home.
You leave your hair straight now.
Childless, your body holds together,
the right clothes have found you,
your face has fallen into place.
You are working on an understanding with God.

Being with you is a sad Christmas;
you show me the present
then put it back into the drawer.
I remember the theory,
to have something properly I must be able to let it go.

You said that like the White Witch in *Alice*
I did everything backwards.
The blood, the scream and only then
I pricked my finger.
Perhaps by the time you are really gone
I won't feel a thing.

No Dice

We met up in Parliament Square by the left-hand lion.
His hair was down his back,
tall and skinny, a pied piper in brown and khaki.
He liked facts and knew millions of them
about Art and Films.
I picked up his intonations
and quoted him verbatim.
We were both impressed.
I hid myself from him, the things I couldn't bear
so that we both believed, eventually,
I was his own creation.
He walked two steps ahead.
Now and then, when my real and miserable self got out
and I sulked and wouldn't do as I was told,
he slapped me.
A great joker, he offered lemonade
and brought a glass of spirit vinegar.
He laughed at all my efforts and called me Pumpkin
but wouldn't let me go.

Six weeks before the wedding
I said no dice.
I looked in the mirror at the cheesecloth frock
and thought what a long time

till death would part us.
Mother returned the presents and consoled him.
I had always been wilful
perhaps I would come round in time.
It was a mean trick
just before his finals.
Better than divorce or the bread knife.
He took no permanent harm
and later married someone more obliging.
I held off, needing time
and a few more facts.

Field

The field of oilseed rape
is printed cotton cloth
bordered with high hedge.
Moist yellow and green laid down for the background
then, while the dye is still wet,
drips of red
so the mouths of the poppies open.
Those flowers are the times of love between us
how they shout
on the quiet cloth of marriage where we live.

Starting School

Before we got you off to school
the days were all a rosary;
round and round
we filled in the laborious days
with sleeps and shopping and sandwiches.
It was life inside a walnut shell
small scale and airless,
school has tapped it open.

You like it all,
except the toilet seats which are vicious
and some of the bossy girls.
The bustle sweeps you away
and we come to take home what's left.

Too tall for baby cuddles
you sit wrapped in a towel on my knee and wail
'How can I love you with all this going on?'
I help with your pyjamas
hoping that the right things in the right order
will be some comfort to you
as they are to me.

Caterpillar

Charlotte was dug out of my body
an early potato
she slept a lot at first
as if nothing had happened.
I couldn't do much for her anyway
with a wound like the cleft in a peach
spectacularly bruised.
I was rather overdone with flowers.
I lay and watched a small green caterpillar
work his way slowly
around the frilled lips
of the sweet peas you brought from our garden.
The florist's sprays were grand
and made a good screen
but the caterpillar kept me close to home
and said things that you couldn't
in the clean ward
under the eye of the clock.

Ashes

We haven't spoken of it since the early days
when I came to you like a half wild cat
looking for a warm place to winter.
What I wanted then was my cannister of ashes
thrown onto the oily sea from the end of a stone pier,
to join the pull and heave forever.

I have changed my mind.
There should be ashes but I want them to go home
to the slope of churchyard
with your grandfathers.
When the tattoos of my flesh are dust in a pot
I will be anchored and still.

A Nest of Hats

You kept your hats, a fine assortment,
in their bags and boxes in a heap
between the high double bed and the window.
I was happy in your flat, festooned with plastic flowers,
the sixty years between us made for peace.
You ran my bath and brought me cups of tea
and I listened to the endless talk about the past,
a web of people I didn't know.
In bed we joked about falling into the nest of hats
and giggled long after we should have been asleep.
In the night I stopped my own breathing to check on yours.

You lasted out for years;
some in the flat, some in the upstairs room at mother's.
Falling out of bed wasn't funny,
two of us hauled you back in, your legs like a mermaid.
In the final coma you lay snoring
right through your birthday
and then died.
With all the routine palaver finished I am glad to find
that the hats are gone but the joke stands.

Wythop Mill

Overshot,
the wheel catches water in its pockets
with a flish, flish, flish.
Through the wall along the axle
in a stone wet room
the metal teeth go racketing round and round
driving the belts that drive the saw bench and the lathes.
There is no mechanism to throw it out of gear,
only if the water stops, the wheel stops.
Somewhere in its turning is a tight spot
that slows all the movement in the wheel, cogs, whistling belts.
Past it, a frantic, rattling race to make up time.
Between us we have had a sticky place
where there seemed, momentarily, no way forward.
Freed from that fear
the water runs
the wheel turns.

God and the Holy Stones

Instead of Lent I have been feasting
on holy stones and sea.
The wind always finds the abbey on the cliff at Whitby,
eating the columns, planing the rock.
At Riveaulx I trod the day stairs
and the night stairs of the monks dorter,
walked alone up the aisle of the roofless amazed church.

My church on Easter Sunday
is suburban and grey, plain and cold.
Rows of camel-coated ladies draw their kneelers to them
and stand to sing lamely about graves and kings.

God lives in our house
in a fossil pebble in the drawer of the sewing machine in the hall.

Union

I am a tree on the margin,
the soil thin under me,
my leaves followed soon by dearth and silhouette.
You are solid, all through the same tight grain of stone,
held in the earth.
The union was expedient;
you would share the bud and air,
I your tenancy of the real ground.
I have grown over the hard edge slowly,
the seam of wood and stone is no longer clear
and the plane of our joining, invisible,
is an unexpected glory, I rejoice.

The Gap

After five years maternity leave
I come home to myself
walking fast away from the school.
The seagull's cry is a baby.
In the kitchen I switch on anything
to stop the running quiet;
their voices kept me in place and the silence scrambles me.
The heat has gone from the waterbottles,
the dents in the pillows are plumped out.
There are no more snatched moments of peace
while they jump on their beds,
I can stand for a long time looking out
at the frost shadow of the house
where the sun hasn't reached.

Maggie Hannan

MAGGIE HANNAN was born in Wiltshire in 1962 and lived in Derbyshire before moving to Cumbria in 1985. She has worked as a monumental mason and as a life model. Some of her poems were published in *No Holds Barred* (Women's Press 1985) and broadcast on the BBC. She won an Eric Gregory Award in 1990, and was recently awarded a Writer's Residency at the Tyrone Guthrie Centre by Northern Arts. ●

ACKNOWLEDGEMENTS: *The Gregory Anthology 1987-1990* (Hutchinson, 1990); BBC Radio Cumbria.

Coming Down from Derry Hill

During my sister's birth
you were at the cinema
watching Bardot, I think,
or was it Monroe?
Ploughing your blonde hair
with a huge hand and packing
tobacco in a pipe.

You kept mink then
and fed them on tripe.
It stank,
mingling with the sweet
stench of litter and
dank musk of mink.
I clung onto you –

Baggy-trousered Dad,
my hand fisted in yours,
tiptoeing slyly past rows
of pinch-faced creatures
curled in whorls against wire
like furred snails.
You gave them no names.

I saw you leave the shed
swinging a brace of mink
doll-bodied and loose
like cats in ample skins,
and a door shuttering
to and fro; a whiff of gas
sloughed off in the breeze.

Coming down from Derry Hill
to our cottage – you'd enter
gladly, sprawl yourself,
all legs and fingers
tapping to the Beatles
or jazz, and wink at me once
from the black chair.

The Lamper
(for Sally & John)

Black clad and mithered he harries his weight
down the gulley, a yard in ten flushed out,
limited now to a strobe beat: no sound
save an undertone of blood. Still between
cover and water, he checks – no echoed
beam – tips darkly towards the edge, spilling
his limbs in deeper, spanning the lit pool.
Bracing one leg against a half-sunk car...
almost too soon for steadying...he traps
a fish in the freeze-frame, slips the net's end
slowly under, jemmies out his salmon.
Later, driving home, his conversation
idles on the seaward journey of grilse;
then, bored, he turns on the CB, relays
his code-name as 'The one that got away'.

Inmates

The boy yell, bull elephant charge
of sound: a dead-pan sift of noise
through the ward to staff quarters.

Caroline's having a fit in perfect treble.
Butterfly convulsions. She propels herself
like wind-up Donald Duck capsized.

'I'm going to HANG myself' says Mark,
but temporarily is satisfied with
stretching his neck as far

as it will go up the chimney. Lying
crucified in the grate his trousers
stain with the thrill of extension.

Sitting together during Recreation,
she concentrates, shifts her tits
nervously inside a cheap print dress

like a female impersonator at the
Rotary Club party. He pats his breast
pocket wherein lie six inches of string:

a tight possibility balled against
his heart. They discuss whether it's enough,
whether you could hang on so much.

Tom Passey's Child

Unremarkable at first, this infant,
bedded down and silent in a cot,
fingers shoaling at the blanket's edge –
'Hold him' – I hesitate, cautious
of what might be discovered, then
some instinct draws my hand to his.

The grip's not right, tensile –
he begins the search for focus
and fails, staring up as if through
depths of water –
I reach down for him:
the shock of his weightlessness.

The stillness of his gaze!
Held close, his breathing's fierce
and sharp against my cheek,
the effort precocious. Like this
Tom Passey finds us, transfixed,
all things fallen quiet at his exposure.

Tom's deliberate clatter at the sink,
his leaving for the garden, the words
'His sickness sickens me also'.
Outside he is quickly busy,
a thumbprint marking every seedling,
bedded down and silent in the ground.

Tap

There are even silences, prosecutors
of the auricle to bring charges
against bunched cartilage. Here,

we are the captives of the peripheral
nerves. Cauliflower, jug or shell-like
conjoin with the mechanical synapse,

a telephone flyblown with voices –
Grapevine, Talkabout, Chatline.
3 a.m. and the plastic is pressed

to the lobe, mole-like. Tones dust
the inner drum like a moth glass-trapped.
Hearsay. Static. Molecules become

alphabets and into ear, malleus
and incus at it like Punch's truncheon –
hammering and hammering

the cochlea, coiled and recoiled.
The tongue upstarts – jumps
and flicks each outbreathed breath

to word: unleashing a thesaurus.
What is moot is *polyglot,*
medley, Babel 61 n. confusion.

The Bone Die

Even the wrist's fast jack
is funked by a thumb's rub,

chances and freaked odds
of plane, pit, dot and dot

are pocketed or scuttled:
a weathered die contrives

its craft of luck from years –
edges all unwhet, or honed

in captivities of palm. Thrown
down for a free run (an ack-ack

clatter after gulling) it's pulling
up dead on a rising surface,

and jinxes still by a worn slant:
two up, two up, where fractures web

the sockets of its eyes – askance –
laugh lines – a probability of chaos.

Seq

1 *Was*

Inescapable: to start with the history
of a place or a thing, people – circumstances.

Take, for instance, the way a shadow's hinged,
how it meets a wall, stands upright less than a person is.

I suppose the was of it – of them – was what
I overheard, a half-shadow or, perhaps,

the story like a swimmer seen from somewhere up;
a surface and a kick or flap, then gone. She was

saying how she'd found herself that day (they weren't
speaking), before a mirror – God knows how –

with one hand pleasuring herself. But what of her other
hand? She'd seen it scribbling the glass,

her features uglied to grimace, *all cock-eyed,*
she said, *like he was, over me.* She came.

2 *Is*

In her absence, he
acts strangely. He is frisking
the space where she was.

Holding a pubic
hair in thumb and forefinger;
retractable vice.

A detective! No.
A shaman: he eats the hair,
he sees her image.

3 *Ago*

All night they had watched the slow
arc of a star, a satellite's
tracing of the galaxy.

On earth, the unthinkable: he'd lost
his mind. He sensed it falling past him
like sycamore seeds as he made love to her.

She opened her eyes just as he pulled
his face awry: they came together,
naked, resembling each other.

4 *Meanwhile*

Dog-eared, genial, days pad through the house
following a sinew of fragrance. Full
now, the memory needs no flowers, twines
of clematis; what is anoints itself.
Passing and becoming annihilate
the world. Look, a toy train shuttles away
from the valley. An insect balances
on the wine's meniscus. A cat cyphers
contentment on the windowsill. Measured
like this it's a time of perpetual ease,
snapshot, moment of grace or gracelessness.
A touch insinuates such radiance
and pulls away; there's no need for others.
Overheard. A half-shadow. Or. Perhaps.

Geoffrey Holloway

GEOFFREY HOLLOWAY was born in Birmingham in 1918. He joined the RAMC in 1939 and later served with a parachute field ambulance corps. After qualifying as a social worker at Southampton University he spent the rest of his career in the field of mental health, chiefly in Cumbria. He has published many books of poems, including *Rhine Jump* (London Magazine Editions, 1974), which was a Poetry Book Society Choice, and *All I Can Say* (Anvil Press, 1978). A volume of new and selected poems will appear from Littlewood Press in 1991. ●

ACKNOWLEDGEMENTS: Geoffrey Holloway: *All I Can Say* (Anvil, 1978); *London Magazine* and *Poetry Now* (BBC Radio 3).

Non-Accidental Injury Slides

Mostly it happens in the first year.
Tender flesh, hardened lash.

This was a belt. Two marks –
the smaller the buckle.

This one was strangled. You can't tell;
bruising was inside.

This horseshoe bite needs checking,
against family mouths.

Cigarette burns, these.
Get to them quickly, they fade.

Space – repeat – space your X-rays.
Fractures can be shy.

These children are briefed never
to say a thing. That is, if they can speak.

These children won't cry.
Only their wounds are attention-seeking.

These children are watchful.
What they have seen, they see.

The Lovers

It would be easier if they were on
a cinema screen; one could absorb them.
Here on this station platform
the feeling's faintly voyeuristic.
Though why is enigmatic: these
are only naked with happiness.
A dangled scarf and a pair of high heels –
they look to be seventeen, no more.
She flutters off to a sweet machine,
falls on him like a sunbeam,
feeds him chocolate neat as a bird.
He takes her into the haven of his smile,
hands on shoulders rocks her gently,
as a lazy tide a boat.
And now she's crowded into his arms again,
stippling his face with quick, light kisses.
Explosive as a Samurai sword
the northern flier slices past.
It could be a breeze, the notice it gets.
Why are they travelling? We don't know.
What they're waiting for they already have.

Things

The tin bath once brimmed with daughters,
the dislocated axehelve, and the trunk
of the plum-tree that wouldn't burn –
it's all there, by the disused shed
whose rivets shove out like mushrooms,
whose chipped stones are web-hoary –
moult of some random, long-haired cat.
We could have it moved, all of it. But won't.
Ruin has its own mana,
the seasoned credit of the personal.
We'll be neat as nothing soon enough –
but no one's tipping the dustman yet.

The Virtue of Slovenliness

We had an old door
roofing
the coal bunker,
but it rotted,
weather-bust.

So now
there's only
a concrete rectangle,
black scree,
and in an odd crack
the dandelion.

Every spring
(and more)
it flowers;
every winter
snaps...
(runaway chunks,
seismic slides,
whatever).

It's been
a corky wart
two months now,
but today I see
it's cheeky as always –
inching out
into sallow,
mucky leaf.

And that white, carrotlike root
will be somewhere underneath, probing –
the fat, inner-tubey stalk
flashing its cocky, common head...

Now if I was one of those fixit guys,
mail-order segments fitting together
in a dapper, blueprint dream –

insulated, waterproofed,
with a flap door craftily inserted,
and the coal only so far to the door...

it couldn't have lived.
Nor I.

Bash on Basho:
Six of the Best

Cubist
Spring. The golfball head
of the Dutch philosopher
is a plum blossom.

Surreal
Spring. On the bald head
of the Dutch philosopher
a cherry blossom.

Sexy
Spring. On the bald head
of the thinker no toupet.
Only a Dutch cap.

Trompe l'oeil
Spring. The thinker's head
says hello Dali I'm a
Dutch interior.

Monty Python
Spring. Teeheeing off,
the Dutch philosopher's head
becomes a birdie.

Feminist
Spring. The Dutch thinker
is checkmated by guess who –
a hairy Duchess.

Hypochondriac

He's had

imaginary hepatitis
glaucoma
St Vitus

imaginary septicaemia
beri beri
haemolytic anaemia

imaginary furunculosis
itching anus
Korsakoff's psychosis

imaginary hordeolum
trick knee
spastic colon

but has last arrived safe and sure
– so the current report is –
at the perfect cure

imaginary rigor mortis

A Hand for Some Others

He didn't, no he didn't think continually
of those inscribed as 'great':
homage-touted in the modish weeklies,
town-cried by dons and dandies as 'significant'
– daisies strutting as sunflowers;
more often of those whose allotments were slighter,
scribblers the mandarins didn't rate
but whose tensions, gustos, were demonstrably his own
– students with tercets shoved under their notebooks,
workmen nursing a stanza through lunch breaks,

housewives awake to a fleeting, small hours cadence –
who sometimes missed it, trying too hard,
sometimes half-got it, were sometimes so right;
who shared a language of quirks, fury, weakness,
talked, wrote as equals, might bitch a bit
but would cut out each other's truths to stick on the wall;
who unobtrusively but fiercely cared
about the tuck of a line, the fit of an image;
who were supposed to die in small magazines
– but didn't.

Indian Rope Trick

Silence. Noon. The tower of sun, its rapt, circled crowd.
Central they stand: the stripped fakir in his tall, snailshell turban;
the chosen boy, in a twist of loincloth, the borrowed, sacred mongoose
        in his hands.
The man bows assent to sun, then splaying hands exact as a conductor's
stares tense as a burning glass at cracked, immediate earth.
And from that dusty foot of ground it comes,
from the risen evocative crescendo of his hands:
a rope white-taut as a king python, charismatic, determined.
The mongoose runs, the boy leaps, locks thighs over, clinches feet,
begins to swarm; proud, deliberate.
And it grows with him, that white snake, every stretched handhold
        surer, firmer,
till lost eyes tipped back below see pink, clinching soles go lighter,
fade, dissolve into that white stalk, that taut irreversible taper...
till there is no mast of shadow sloped from the watchers' forgotten
        feet,
only the trick that's never done:
the sky blue and plate-bare but for a vapour trail of sloughed skin;
in the distance like a sidling leaf what could be a slipped loincloth –
in the ring a crosslegged veteran at prayer,
and a turbaned youth walking off with a bright-eyed mongoose on his
        shoulder.

Monitors

Across the ward green biros of monitors
compete for Sister's eye:
one switchbacked daft as the Road Runner,
the other rippling evenly: a child's drawing of waves.
My locker's a surreal tip:
GET WELL cards from the kids, boldly misspelt
(earwigs, dogs, caterpillars wreathing
and peering round the capital L's)
next to a bowl of pinks, the peripatetic urinal.
When they came to see me the day after
I splurged into cliché: 'Thank God you're here!';
blaspheming, slobbering my well-kept image,
letting myself disgracefully (but thankfully) down.
They are thinning my blood with rat poison;
the syringe driver at my wrist confirms it.
Twelve hours, it will whine from nowhere,
a mosquito-bleep, wanting a refill, more.
When I told him I felt something there –
more than a twinge at the top of the testing breath –
the dapper auburn Consultant checked,
reading the spoor of his stethoscope round nipples, chest.
'Aye, there's the pleural rub, gentlemen' –
leaving his white-smocked gaggle to hear it too.
They gave me morphia that night, from the zonker's trolley,
its wash leather wiped me clean;
I shone like a new window, for six hours.
That one by the door came in yesterday,
ruckling like someone spading up snow on gravel,
coughing from clinker-grey to beetroot.
They clapped a respirator on him. Against those pillows
he's beaky as a puffin in a chalk niche –
that is, when he doesn't throw it away
to hiss like a gas leak.
Sometimes they screen us off, for no apparent reason –
then show us it: the empty bed.
They tell me the pain will go. Will it? Will it?
Their hands, their optimistic hands.

Old Man

Hairs rush out of his nose and ears
nails jut like windshields

he gabbles confidentially
but names tease him like magicians' cards

bluetits are exploding round
the red nut sock beyond his sill

he looks through them
like a meths drunk

an elder brother's
still hiding his clobber

he scrabbles hours under furniture
for things he had perfectly minutes before

has to crane to hear – and what comes through
is rhymed rhubarb

someone like his old headmaster
is shoving him along a corridor
by the back of his neck

each shuffling step pushes
his head down further

like a drunk's under a tap

his body is beginning to slump
on the iron hook of his neck

he can see himself
falling into the fire

dead meat

if it were only that

Ford Castle: The Borders

afternoons of dove-slurred languor

incense cedars

cropped lawns

what lived
is

out of the stalking museum

mnemonics

instruments:

vizored alcove

wall-set pike

kingly sword   dagger   under glass

stone from a French Queen's finger

who lived
are

legendary principals

flesh of war:

the king impatient for honour and suicide
his longhaired dream taking out the Turks

the castle's lady,
stroking his pleasure for battle plans

the standard bearer
waving victorious truth

the earl helped gingerly down
from his litter of seventy years

to mastermind a subtle fording

who meshed
tore

sequelae

interim payments:

the king with his triple accolade
of fatal wounds

the lady among burnt walls

the standard bearer
his flag of truth wrapped secretly about him

the earl wiping his hands on Scotland's guts

who served
lost

incidentals

vulgar fractions

shoeless jocks   Bannockburn shouting
from their deaf eyes

shattered limeys   bone-weary
too weak to hold their loot

the brave of both nations

a field

of

wet broken clods

owls   gules

      starlit bones

        trumpets

over   Flodden

David Lindley

DAVID LINDLEY was born near Wakefield in 1946 and read History at Cambridge. Until recently he was Tutor-Organiser in West Cumbria for the Workers' Educational Association, teaching courses in literature and music. Currently he is writing a travel book about a journey along the Islamic borders of Southern Europe. ●

Nearness

Feathers fan the spade.
He's back, I think,
And see him perching on a clod,
Head ticking off the time he waits
Until the autumn dig turns up
A palatable worm.
Now he's gone but still in sight
His double flies in from the south, dips
In passing at the earth
And gives place to a third.

Since he is three or more, and maybe she,
Should I settle for an it
To stand for all the redbreasts
That have ever perched
To see us humans do their work for them?

Yet three persist, just three,
Distinct in habit
I should like to take for personality.
Proximity's the index.
The third that's never less than yards away.
The second scarcely here before he's gone.
Only the first comes near enough
To have me more than measure him,
So near I call him bold.

I try to read him,
Reach him with my glance.
I fancy as he edges in I have.
But what he makes me see
Is how he eats –
How his black eye calibrates the girth
Of anything that stirs,
Head ticking off, not time, and least of all
The time of day, but any chance
Too big a grab.
And then the stab.

It's good as gone.
While feathers heave the way
We'd heave to vent our food, not swallow it,
Only the tail's red tip curls still
As if it were his tongue.

A snatch of piping from the hedge.
This also might be his
Were he not otherwise engaged
Wrestling his inward worm.
He wins at last.
And I could foster thoughts
Of serpents vanquished
Or of things sent down some universal path
Of sacrifice and metamorphosis
But for this cheerful nearness
He insists on.

The tongue, thank God, is swallowed down.
But something in his throat,
Some function of the slow subsiding heave of him
Bespeaks the perfect nearness and sufficiency
Of gullet to the thing it's gorged on.

Relief when stirrings
Make me turn my collar, him his feathers, up;
When airy something makes us neighbours,
Feeling both the nearness of the winter's maw.

Fennel

What did we wish from you?
Vegetable hearts. To snip you off
At fluted arteries.
Chop your bulbous celery for spice:
Sweet slice for salad, flattery for fisl

Exotic of the umbelliferae,
What, in a season such as this,
Could we expect?
Faint fountain plumes on bolting stalks.
Thin tubes piped out from stunted ventricles.

Snap them. Fell them. Crush the root.
And air's sweet aniseed,
Cumbrian dank is balmy dry.
Conspiracy of nose and eye has
Lank sheeps of Sicily bow their heads
To browse the yellow knots of broken herbage.

They tell truly why
We grew you.

Curly Kale

A bush of loo brush
Or of fringed green loofah.
Crunches like coral.
Bunched brackets of brassica.
And all the while the riddler rhymes,
    Pickings for pigeons.

Potato Blight

The tops were sign enough,
Bent sticks dying in midlife.
But when the first root came up,
A clutch of stinking pusbags,
At that the garden rows ran out
All over Ireland.

A Marxist to Liberals
(1968)

When he entered
Pilgrims huddled in the aisles,
Toe to spine. The smiles
He flashed in transit to the rostrum wintered
To a bitter line between the hair
Of lip and goatee beard. The bare
Brown pate and brandished finger
Promised us a glimpse
Of what it was to watch, if not to hear,
Lenin speak.

He held us for an hour in silence.
Silence tightened
Not by duty, patience or by bodies frightened
Into immobility despite their aches and cramps,
But silence given by attention
To the ring, the sense, the worth
Of what he told us:
'Socialism will engulf the earth.'

He finished, and we clapped.
And he received his due reward
With smiles and waves, evidently satisfied
That we should show a sympathy wide
Enough to harbour him, and wide
Enough to meet him with mere fascination
For yet one more opinion.

By Fire or Flood

What's so drastic in the Germans
Makes them want to die in flame –
Goethe with his blissful longing,
Wagner's twilight gods the same?

Nothing less than this will do them –
Burn to death and so become.
Meanwhile gentler English yearning
Contemplates a watery doom.

Maggie drifting on the river.
Wild waves beckon little Paul.
Alfred Lord. Phoenician sailor.
All await the Pilot's call.

Is it merely choice of method,
Just as well be rope or knife?
What unites the thing that matters –
Sickness unto death of life?

The Cryptogram

The trailing pen draws out a seismograph
Of self, it's said, the lower loops alone
Enough to give away a tide of passion
Never felt as yet, or acted on.
Another glimpse of glory in the name
We're tagged with, wherewithal to prove, when
Truth is told, we're stuff that's come from kings (ten
Generations back), or genius, or madmen.
Best chance of all, the self celestial:
Our ruling star a twinkling glass that both
Burned in some secret figure at our birth
And serves as now the lens to read it with.
Sciences of soul and dark inheritance,
Lend us the hope that clodhoppers might dance.

Cromwell: The Last Portrait
(a footnote to Marvell)

A miniature in brass-rimmed frame,
As if to shrink the greatest name
   And bind it in a ring
   Of small men's fashioning.

Except that those half-shuttered eyes
Which on distance used to gaze
   Seem rested on the air
   Within the picture's sphere.

Or if they stray beyond the glass
They light on Nature's emptiness
   Where History makes room
   And other spirits come.

Despite the armour's pitted plate,
The badge of wars ordained by Fate,
   The man it cases here
   Is instrument no more.

He chiefly offers to our care
A wispy head of fading hair
   And asks of us no crown
   To mask Time's work undone.

Charles McDonald

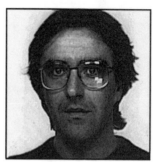

CHARLES McDONALD was born in Darlington in 1957. He studied English at North Staffordshire Polytechnic and was later unemployed for five years. He now works in the Probation Service in Carlisle. ●

Fresh Mussels

Blue as a new moon midnight
And sprayed with crusts of brindled coral
A pound of mussels
Lies in an earthen bowl of cold water
Refreshed by a dribbling tap.

I slip my hand in smoothly
Picking out a gnarled shell
And set to work with an old knife.
It's easy to chip away sea-life
And coarse grains of sand –
Finer specks take patience.

Scraping, dipping, cleansing,
And marine begins to flake
Revealing lighter tints
On tiny corrugations.
Winkling silt from the cleft,
Clipping the wisp of beard.

Each mussel gets
A shade less care and attention

Than the one chafed clean before.
Nostrils sicken of the brine,
Hands go numb and patience ebbs.
I shoal them into a pan.

In boiling water the shells whisper open
Giving up soft curls of gold.
When scooped from their shallow beds
And pitched onto my taste-buds
The mussels first hint of delicacy,
And prompt a word of favour,
Then slowly come to cloy the tongue
And query my devotion.

Oxford Gardens

In fifty-nine
What's left of the grass
Shelters the stump of ash
From our wild husbandry.

Broken milk bottles wink
Under a twisted metal chair.
Burnt building-bricks
Tramline the patch of barbecued earth.

Soil is piled in the dustbin.
Lacerated plastic bags,
Trickling tin-cans and vegetable-peelings,
Lump against it.

A 1000cc Kawasaki
Stands padlocked to the concrete post
Which has changed its supporting role
Since neighbours stole the washing-line.

Now a thick wooden gate,
Cobbled together
From an old shed's timber,
Keeps the kids out.

The garden of sixty-one,
Where Mrs Kaur in her golden sari
Scatters bread on the garage roof,
Hosts dozens and dozens of sparrows

Which swoop from emerald apple trees
To feed in a constant chattering.

Nightfishing

Near high tide
Two boys had built a windbreak of pebbles
And lit a small fire of driftwood
For comfort.
A tepee of sticks held their rod
And a line looped into the black water
Which unpeeled in white crashes
At their camp's edge.

We huddled in a pre-war shelter
Some yards up the beach, and watched –
Our bodies not touching,
Our minds feeling out.

As the first drifts of a sea-fog rose to the north
The sky hung full.
Silently, we played join-the-dot‹
Trying to find the *Plough*.
In the obscuring depths
It was hard to make connections.

The fish would not bite
And the fire died.
Still the boys kept on,
Content with the embers,
Certain their luck would change.

In the shelter
Conversation came in waves
And slipped back, changing little.
We were searchers.

Steadily, an old man
Carrying a halogen lamp
Ground his path across the shingle.
A little way off he unpacked reels and tackle,
Piecing them together.
As he fished
The lamp haloed his body.
We took in his practised cast;
The boys ignored him.

A cold offshore wind
Tried to dislodge us
But we all stayed on
Safe on our islands,
Facing the sea,
Nightfishing.

At the Gwen John Exhibition

The canvas squares
Were quite compact,

Pinpointing odd
Images. Quiet

Drawing-rooms,
A gentle light,

Models posing
Soft, silent

Problems. These
Portraits stood alone

Yet, like diary notes
Among unmarked

Pages, patchworked
Gwen John

Body
And soul.

Asdrubral Jiménez

Asdrubral Jiménez has not disappeared.

Frightened cocaine barons and political maggots
In Medellin, Colombia have tried to unstitch him
But Asdrubral has kept the threads together.

They shot him four times
And when he lay in hospital,
Determined to breathe,
They would have shot him four more times
Had he not been guarded
By gunmen loathe to let him die
Unless they wanted it.

Señora Jiménez had a miscarriage.

On the plantations the peasants
Tackled the banana harvest,
Remaining stony-faced
And on the fit-to-work side of starving.

Union leaders in Medellin
Stand like corporals in Passchendaele.

They would have shot him eight more times
Had friends not bribed a pilot
To fly him into exile – out of sight
Not out of mind.

In the T and G, in Cecil Street, in Carlisle
Asdrubral Jiménez sits to applause,
With one bullet still in a lung
And paralysed in one leg
And his crutches on one side.

Translated from the Spanish, his story,
His will not to disappear,
Bequeathes to the few dozen assembled
An insight into the meaning of great words –
Those puffed so casually from our overblown mouths –
That questions even our right
To line up before him.

And then Asdrubral smiles
At his wife,
Shy in the front row,
Another proud exile.

Cheers

Suppose you slosh gin deep into a glass,
Forgetting lemon wedges, icy chunks,
And bolt the doors until the moon has passed,
Kick off your shoes, relax on jumbled banks
Of pillows, quickly sip a dozen drinks
And taste the fiery edge to cut your thirst,
Then take great gulps and caterwaul for yonks
On love's sour cocktail and then roundly curse
The day we met; suppose you do all that
And slump into a stupor, your innards
Half-pickled with alcohol, your ego bruised,
Don't think when you awake, washed with sweat
And flaking, I'll unsay the stinging words
Or take back one sharp jot of pain I've caused.

David Morley

MOIRA CONWAY

ACKNOWLEDGEMENTS: David Morley: *Releasing Stone*, *A Belfast Kiss* and *Mandelstam Variations* (details opposite); *Antigonish Review*, *Bête Noire*, *Echo Room*, *Encounter*, *The Gregory Poems*, *London Magazine*, *Quadrant*.

DAVID MORLEY was born in Blackpool in 1964. He read Zoology at Bristol University and wrote a Ph.D. on environmental science at London University. Before moving to Sheffield, he lived at Bowness, from where he carried out a research programme into the impact of acid rain on Cumbrian lakes and tarns. In 1989 he won a major Eric Gregory Award.

He has published three books of poems, *Releasing Stone* (Littlewood, 1989), *A Belfast Kiss* (Smith/Doorstop, 1990), and *Mandelstam Variations*, (Littlewood, 1991). His work is included in *Poetry Introduction 7* (Faber, 1990). He has held residencies in many schools, and has just published a handbook on writers and artists in schools, *Under the Rainbow* (Bloodaxe Books/Northern Arts, 1991). ●

On Fire

When, on withering into life, smoke
chances on opacity, there

seems a kind of rock
cut from the sharpest energies

in fire: a compliancy, a pliant stone
of smoke, a broken form

turned blunt-end to the ground...
Stoking-up, you flesh that sparse

contracted source. The flame-points swell
with wings and cobbled smoke.

Masking a fist, you weave-in half-burnt wood –
tuff of lichens to fissure in fire –

and stand away, watching how
the falling-up of heat

quarries air of flakes and finity.

A sculptor works less openly,
releasing stone in secret,

scraping through caves to find a captive,
hands like drills. The binds of stone

shrivel to his touch: a plying flame
as fumbles out of smoke. He makes

his fist a phoenix; hands he turns
are wings that clench a fire,

a beak that bites
is chisel in this stone...

The warm wings lift
a trembling limb from rock:

a dust, like smoke, veers into air.

Errand

I came to a place where buildings were going up;
biscuits of slate sat wrapped in twine.
Earth moved like sugar, boiling
against the metal of a dumper.
A machine dropped, dropped its yellow snout,
nuzzling at joists
it hammered-in.
When I got to my father I would learn
the heat of that impact, how you might
light paper from it two hours on...
The air meanwhile would shiver with fire,
a fineless dust, the shouts of impact.

He was with the welders –
short-term hire – cutting thin plate
to microns. Not visored, he
stood out from that coven

of kneeled and sparking men
like something they were making
or melting to start over.
We went out to sandpiles, pounded stone,
his eyes spindling, his mouth
asking and asking why I was there.

Metal-work

The lathe we were at
kept cutting-out
in little deaths;
our anger slid.

Under a blade
sheet-metal split.
I stood where
my father stood me:

this side of a lathe.
Weathers of dust
fell to a hush
at my feet.

I did what he asked:
watched calipers twitch,
legs skinny,
an avocet's;

but looked beyond:
to drill-heads primed,
fluted like wands
of steel.

He halved the work:
held mandrels, clamp.
Drills spoke for him,
talked themselves out.

Air Street

Deer-tracks – I followed them: made
a forest slide through a deer's eye; felt

for myself the trodden dints of hoof,
shorthand codes cut on the frost...

Pitch of night: insurgent shrews
scatter in dissidence between owls.

My torch-beam welds them to the ground;
I could gather them like moss.

The air as well, corrupt with movement,
walks with me like gravity

and, step-by-step, it flenses sound
to whispers of a deer-cut.

Where the tracks street together –
passes of a scalpel –

with torch-light off, eyes wide for catlight,
I read their musks like creosote

and saw the deer – a herd of ten –
scent me there, *and go.*

Morning took me southwards; levelled on fat
curving rails, restive station platforms,

ticks of rain. As if trespassing
I cut the close-wire of people.

Gundogs grabbed me at traffic-lights.
Gamekeepers in Downing Street

met my stare.
It was night delivered me this:

a street lit by nothing –
near where I could sleep –

with a name like nothing: *AIR*.
And I walked it without torch-light

sensitive for the wear of previous creatures.

Exact Fares

Even now, angle-poised over a desk
he takes his cue from the barbiturate
of what was seen. Remembering rain:
how a single droplet breaks its back
on the hurrying window of a No. 3 bus.
Or the fly: simmering on vibrated glass,
intellectual, in that spiderless prison...
A man in corduroys unscrews a flask
and shares warm tea with a woman he hated.
He does not see a fly browse on the brim
of their plastic mug, or the way raindrops garrotte
the nerves of his rheumatic wife. We are sick
with fear the drunk will miss his stop,
lolling over the seatback, leaving it our decision.

Jerusalem

Ballymurphy painted white, inside and out;
road-blocked suburbs, then the accomplishment
of a bounding wall to stop the desert's
abstract itch. This achieved, we grew fluent

in our dialogues: the limit on sense
was vox pop, as was ambivalence
about a noun for boredom. Came the day
a master of lexicography

motorbike-jumped the lower wall-sectors
and made off for the border. He was taken alive,
displayed in the central archives
(after public vasectomy and grammar –

confiscation), writing, rewriting
in blackened sand, *Lift up your hearts and sing.*

The Politicisation of the North Wind

We came out safe, under the aspens; wanted
the road south, but winds deflected
our point of reference to the motorway.
A Police Rover winks on its orbit round
an arterial lane. Cobs of leaf-litter give way
to a blackbird's enquiry. Ivy dripfeeds
an oak, as if accidentally. We need
the road south, but accidents are happening.
A rescue party sifts the rubble of falling
leaves; a hand of the law harries us down turn-offs
– its flickered blue flame; a kestrel makes its one-off
bid in a plunging market. We circle a bend
with a sign saying *Motorway Regulations Terminate Here.*
Aspens. Wind. Regulations terminate here.

Enniskillen

There was a speedboat ploughing up Lough Erne,
an activity I thought the local RUC
would take no shine to.
I watched three little grebes make with the rhythm.

Imagine my discomfiture when the boatman waved
then a four-eyed warden told me to push off.
I plucked up my fag-ends, enough, never enough;
followed lager cans to the centre of Enniskillen,

a place, now, infamous as Walsingham, and shrine
to all discomfiture. I felt a lot for a heaven
whose latest queue
still wore their Remembrance poppies
as though they'd just left the nave
where the priest held back, half-listening for – rain.

White, White

1

As if the snow itself were a country
  with pleasure gardens, hotels, religion,
    babyware, and the word yes and the word no.

You enter its capital along paths of slush.
  Signs direct you to the City Elder. Nothing will grow
    under her rule, as Signs will tell you at every corner.

But when she invites you to her Ice Festival
  you will learn to love Slowfreeze and Nightflake,
    her daughters by sunless adoption. Will they dance,

dance with you? Only so slowly unless they melt
  at the heart from a heat of ecstasy. The parquet
    is white, white. You are falling out of life.

Their images are locked in you forever.
  You will carry them, bright on your lips,
    even over oceans, to your own easy gardens.

One night you may wake before dawn,
  walk naked to where the river thaws
    in its grave. Beneath a bridge of smoothest limestone

put your ear against the ear of winter
  listening for a yes, a no. Or touch
    where the words enter the water,

2

do none of these things. Call at the office.
  When someone says yes the answer is no.
    File your dockets in bin bags for burning

at the moment when a stranger rides up in the elevator.
  Meanwhile, talk of weather or the terrible storm damage.
    Avoid words like informer, auditor, police.

There are things in the wall very like ears.
  Their microphones are wonderful as knots in wood.
    Listen, someone can sell you at the slightest notice

with a single nod. So they will come for you
  in the small hours. To snout through your past
    rabid for evidence. To ask you to repeat after them,

yes, yes, yes. Through it all they will help with heat
  to the arms, chest, your white lips. Then, peace,
    a dream of snow, cold hands holding you,

which you love; that lift you to where water
  rushes over your face. Will you dance, dance?
    Only so slowly. Melting, melting.

Answers on a Postcard

Who forked me like compost from my country? Who spat
  in my water, left me diptherial, half alive?
Who shovelled me in a bucket, lobbed me in the shit

with heads of schoolchildren, kulaks, priests?
  Who hoofed up the ground in Red Square? Who
potted corpses? Who was the angel of earthworms,

of the mass grave, the bone-field?
  Who hacked the breasts off the widow?
Who blurted acid across her mouth? Who forced

her head back and cheesewired her throat?
  Who smashed the nails from my fingers?
Who hauled me out, wrestled me under water

until I spewed the answer? Who chewed it all over –
  the ribcage, skull, the spine?
Who spattered my guts over a Collective?

Who ploughed in brain-mulch? Who broke the earth?
  Who found the stench ever so exciting?
Who felt my death essential to their lives?

Mick North

CAROLINE FORBES

MICK NORTH was born in Lancaster in 1958. After working as director of Lancaster Literature Festival from 1984 to 1987, he helped to run the dance in education company Ludus. He now works as a local arts development organiser in Carlisle. He won a major Eric Gregory Award in 1986, and has published two collections of poems, *Throp's Wife* (Jackson's Arm, 1986) and *The Pheasant Plucker's Son* (Littlewood, 1990). ●

ACKNOWLEDGEMENTS: Mick North: *Throp's Wife* and *The Pheasant Plucker's Son* (see opposite); *The Gregory Poems, London Magazine, New Statesman, Stand, Sunk Island Review.*

Poems to My Father

1. *The Weather*

Your hands have work in them like the weather
in a hill. Your thick skin's grown protective:
the creases cracked when you didn't bother
with barrier-creams, or left the gloves off,

a bloody hindrance. Or just because they
didn't tell you, then, that solvents can leach
the suppling oils from human skin: safety
at work came slower than the living wage

you pedalled to from shop to mill then on
to shunting-yard and plastics plant towards
enough and the first car. It wasn't greed
that made you "double-back" from 12 hours 10-

to-10 to 6-to-6 straight through, but her
and me and the roof, and the rainy day
that might've turned up, and a bit to spare
for the sun. Even now Dad, is that why

you still can't stand to miss the forecast
on the box, demanding *Shush* with your ear
cupped in a hand to catch every last
word, your backside almost out of the chair?

2. *The Finger*

You were always your shift's First-Aider:
St John's Ambulance classes every year
to keep your hand in, Rescue Team member
(formed after the chimney fell), blood-donor –
hardly a day off sick yourself until
the hollow bone of your finger-end cracked
like a shell, caught between two barrels.
You couldn't believe it, flat on your back
with a finger! Hospital, operation –
amazed, you told us how they'd scrape a hip,
lift a bit for your digit and graft it on.
Which is how it's done, Dad – you're put to sleep
and given back what's always been your own:
sick-pay and compensation, blood, flesh, bone.

3. *1962*

There's a photo of us in the backs
behind our house: you in railway-issue
greatcoat, cycle-clips, muffler and flat-cap –
comic working-class; 1962,

careful white ink on the stiff black leaf.
Christine Nuttall's sat with her back to the wall,
scratching grit; our Jane's poised above her ball,
ready, begging for a toe to kick it off

the picture into Beaumont Street.
White paint on next-door's cock-eyed gate
spells 84. It's winter, from the trees.
Next-door's floral washing fills in the breeze.

Beyond the white frame, Jack Taylor's polished
black Vanguard waits. Ernie Nuttall's club-foot
bobs him through the rubbish in their smashed
backyard, yelling blue murder...I can't set

down the rest, how that winter came and where
it went; Ernie's still the same and Jack died,
there was a past that became a future –
tell me what fixed us, and how we got outside.

4. *Trio*

    1

Your record cupboard's crammed – all in order,
Composers through to Bands; brass from Fodens,
Grimethorpe, Black Dyke Mills, all the champions,
miners and weavers and factory-hands.
You'd wake me with it, home after night-shifts –
music rising up the stairs in slow drifts
like light brightening behind window-glass.
I've heard it said that working men chose brass
because their hands weren't fit for finer stuff,
that hard labour had made their skin too tough
to sense an ivory or tune a string;
so they spat, and made the rude tubas sing.

    2

You've a fiddle stashed in the glory-hole,
that limbo at the head of the stairwell –
what couldn't be used and couldn't be slung
closeted in darkness, behind the hung
parade of coats and empty shoes. A black case
fogged with dust, the clasps stiff under my braced
thumbs: snug inside, the wood still shone
in its plush mould. A pair of strings'd gone,
the horse-hair bow had slackened – how long
since you worked your old fiddle into song
beyond the always false first note, that screwed
your eyes up as the catgut stretched and mewed?

That's how I think of it: I've never heard
you play the simplest tune, not even cared
to ask you if you would, or could. I've seen
you flexing your accordion between
strapped wrists, for love, for the music in you
wanting to come out – forced down through
a pumping arm to your fingers, searching
the braille of too many buttons. Or perching
on a stool you press out waltzes from an
electronic organ, Reggie Dixon
in your own front room. My joke; but I've seen
the fiddle, shut up like what might've been.

The Pheasant Plucker's Son

In his father's cupped hands
a plump chick nestles, at his feet
the emerald-hooded beauties
nod an eye to spilt grain
and gather to his clucking tongue.

Sir William can't be tekkin any more on
listen if yer want a job to do boy
whistle grandad's old dog out of its sty
an part its hair wi that gun.

His first day at the paper mill
they had him spread across the fent-stacks,
hands on him, knees, a ruck
of limbs and Blinkhoe's big face
still closing on him weeks after,
Eyes like a sheep's twat the bastard, look!
little red veins, raw rims, the mouth said
Go on say it for us, s'easy, SAY it
a hand blacked his balls with grease.

Near the back of the boiler-house
in Wilson's bottom field,
the foreman found him black-taped
to a sapling, smeared prick
winkled through his fly, *Bin raped
ave yer, Wurzel-fuckin-Gummidge?*

                    *

Between Stott's Wood and the river
the guns staked out. Beaters crackle
in the thicket on the first drive.

An hour since he found two crows
trapped in a cage, black wings
batting at the mesh roof.
He teased the sneck up off the door
and propped it open. Two ewes
lay rotting under shitty perches.
The ragged birds went quiet and watched.

Yesterday he took some tea to Mary,
Blinkhoe chopped the sign in his arm's crook
Ey Wurzel ave yer brok yer duck?

Grandad sez They do it to em all
Mary sez Stir yer tea wi it luv
Foreman sez Keep yer eye on that roll

*ah'm not the pheasant plucker
ah'm the pheasant plucker's son
ah sez to mi dad did he know
crows ave black pointed tongues?*

Ordnance Survey in the Northern Counties

The Commissioners believe that everything
is named, that land is branded like a beast
to prove its ownership and pedigree:

a word steps softly on the moss's crust,
inks tease rivers out to becks like blue trees;
my letters stitch their banks from mouth to spring
and thread fine serifs through each mountain gill.

Contours whorl like thumbprints, circling my quill;
I dress the map in crocheted black shawls,
string beads of blood between their strands to plot
these common paths a poor man borrows, sweating
in a rich man's fields to raise good walls;

Without a name to bear him witness, I draw
an apronful of stones to mark his spot.

Shap

The name confronts you –
a wind with a wet slap in it
leathering the fell,

flapping black oilskins,
spitting at squinting eyes.
Ewes bunch at the wall,

the collie slinks low,
scuds between gusts,
blown by the skirling whistle.

Two crows are blots
on fence posts. On barbed wire,
clots and wisps of coarse wool.

White plumes torn from the quarry.
Fieldfares shucked from a thorn tree,
nowhere to settle.

The buzzer blares. The dull boom.
A wind with a clap of thunder in it,
stamping its boot on Shap Fell.

Red Desirée

Saturday morning, Wolverhampton market:
canvas awnings blacken in the wet,
gangways are a mush of straw and squashed fruit.
I stand waiting for potatoes at the stall
that sells potatoes only: queues from each small
cubicle of piled spuds for the best deal
in the square, Javelin and Pentland Dell,
Fir Apple, taties with names like low-level
fighter-bombers, race-horses, the lonesome trail.

She's saying, *Them's waxy and them's floury,*
depends ow you like em – you floury
or waxy? And she winks as her curly
black hair flounces ringlets, and the gold glints
in her ear and one tooth, a smile that hints
at more than potatoes and freezing stints
at the stall with her two rough brothers, men
she's a slave to for three days a week, deafened
by tubers thundering into weighing pans

and thunderous, bullying shouts: NOTHER BAG
OF EDWARDS, NOW! The younger one's back
is a trestle, with a bruised lumpy sack
his brother hoists, then sits it like a child
on the counter. They're both dumped into old
rag-arsed pants and stubbly jumpers; hot and cold
have reddened their skins, razor-blades don't glide
easily on their pocked faces, aren't held
right in raw potato fingers that take pride

in mauling weights and big, hungry scoops.
Her rubber-gloved hand draws open the lip
of my bag, ready; her brown eyes look up
into mine and what she says falls away
under THAT'S IT KEEP EM MOVIN MAGGIE!
and I hear myself asking, *Desirée…*

Pinder

Ice plates the tarn in its hollow,
in the cove where the sun won't go;
under their grey steel hatch
the blind white fish grow thinner.
Trees are where a nail has scratched
the paint off black iron; past them Pinder's
battered tractor bucks the rutted lane
and judders to the flock. Again
and again he's up the fell, arms spilling
fodder, reeling his bitch on the string
of his yell. This morning the beck
was candlewax in the silent ghyll;
the white hare's ghost broke trail, kicked
mist across the snow on Pinder's Hill.

An Account

I paid for the blooding of Hobson's hide
fourpence to the man Miller of Ambleside.
When Hobson my horse threw my eldest, Will,
I gave George Brown of Troutbeck, bone-setter,
half-a-crown. Then when he seemed no better
I fetched Dickinson of Crook, near Kendal,
bone-setter, to look at his thigh; for which
I lost seven-and-six. Towards his charges
in going to London, to get the King's Touch
for the Evil, I lent my brother Roger
a full ten pounds. I fear this is too much
illness to meet; I swear in the ledger
that John Rigg and Elizabeth, his wife,
made cost of this work in the days of their life.

Portrait in a Brass Gong

Monday night was for doing the brasses:
an elephant-bell and two tall candlesticks
twisted like Spanish; a pair of nameless
cylinders that were heavy as bricks

and stood guard each end of the mantlepiece
like castles in chess, a craftsman's wedding-
gift from Grandad; the gong her elbow-grease
could buff to such a polish, that would swing

a disc of flashlight from its sideboard perch
when struck. It stood on a box of cutlery,
oakwood clasped with silver like a High Church
bible; under the lid, treasure slept soundly

in its velvet Royal Blue bed, rubbed up
once in a blue moon and used less often.
The sideboard kept her papers in its club-
footed cupboards, rolled up in a sweet tin

or filed in a shoe-box; a red notebook
full of arithmetic; an old nugget
of brazil nut for tending to scratched wood.
Friday night was 'Office', and Thursday got

a week's wages saved and spent; on Monday
she polished the dinner-gong till it gave
a comic self-portrait and her hands prayed
in her lap, black with Brasso, marriage, love.

M.R. Peacocke

JAMES HOLT

M.R. PEACOCKE was born in London in 1930, and grew up there and in Devon. After many years of married life, bringing up children and working as a teacher, she moved alone to a small hill farm in Cumbria in 1985. She has won prizes in various national poetry competitions, and is the author of *Marginal Land* (Peterloo Poets, 1988).

The speaker in her poem 'The Anatomy of a Horse' is George Stubbs, anatomist and painter of horses, who in 1756 went to live in a remote Lincolnshire farmhouse with his common-law wife, Mary Spencer. There he dissected horses and made studies for the plates of his book, *The Anatomy of the Horse*, which was published in folio in 1766. ●

ACKNOWLEDGEMENTS: M.R. Peacocke: *Marginal Land* (Peterloo, 1988); *Arvon Anthology, Northern Poetry* (Littlewood, 1989), *Poetry Matters* (Peterloo, 1989).

The goddess

We startled each other. She was peering
into a wing mirror, one hand flat
to her lank hair. *Lies*, she said.
*Get it adjusted. And I know you
with your pig Latin and your dog Greek
so none of your excuses. Anyway
on a fixed pension one can't afford
even a three-wheeler. I should have enjoyed
a spin down to Staines. So what,
he's past it.* – and cackled abruptly,
left arm crooked against long breasts.
The responsibility, she said.
*You have no idea of the burden
upon us upon me immortals.
Our times were otherwiser.*
    Leaving a river rankness
she passed the bottle bank and the parked cars
and stalked away through willowherb and creeping thistle
with the furious face of a hen.

At the entrance

Came by sporting a nowhere hat,
guitar on his shoulder.
I thought I just... Hands searching
as though for fee or bribe,
eyes trawling for a shadow that might quake
like candleflame in the darkened hall.

Not in, shaking my human single head.
(Why should imagined loss
hurt like the real thing, and why
his pain become my own?) *Tell her
I just...* and revved away to the somewhere world,
his back nailed taut in leather.

Final reductions

What will become of these, the drab, the harsh,
the sour-coloured, garish,
of sad cloth crudely gathered,
raw-hemmed with hanging thread,
fastened with dull huge buttons, heavy-collared,
drooping on corner racks, each with its affidavit
struck through in red;
the ones twitched over daily
by desultory hands, docketed, cased
in greying flesh finally reduced,
shuffling in rooms and corridors
where a whole summer day
fits a white teacup handed out at three?

In memoriam

and some there be which have no memorial
such as Miss Lattimer whose son was no good
·and whose hope was in the bingo caller.

Heavy Miss Lattimer with the white hand
pigmented in patches, whose large pale eyes
moistened while reading DOG THROWN FROM HIGH WINDOW,

Sally of the swollen knees, jumble sailor
intrepid among charity's flotsam,
what kind of memorial would you have wished?

Your joy was a little bottle of Chypre,
a plastic rose, a tabby cat that has gone
to another place, they say a better

like you, Sally, whom I forget for months
at a time; till arbitrary things – a mop,
a sweet chemist's counter stink – present you
solid as a monument; and then I know
that your name liveth until it's my turn.

Soap

> *(Jottings from the notebook of Herr A. Leo, who in 1672
> sent from Italy to the Lady von Schleinitz a parcel of soap
> with a detailed description of use.)*

Lady, this alabaster...
Having in the course of my travels (Peregrinations?)
Heureux qui comme Ulysse –

Take a bason of soft water.
Moistening between the palms of the hands this...?
Having but little skill, Madam, to

– such ablutions as the most refined life
must occasionally necessitate, even
in our more frigid northern parts.

Parts! Those parts which Actaeon, greatly daring (?)
When chaste Diana, at her bath surprised...
Prized. This gift, though poor, yet prized.

Having observed at the Court of Savona
among those beauties most...Among those hills.
Odorous hills of pearl(!)

Those perfumes most esteemed among Princes.
Arabian princes? Arcadian?
Arcadian shepherdesses!

Those cheeks like unto...
Washed in the (Laved?) I beseech you,
Madam, favourably to –

If in the common parlance

Your Ladyship's most (etc.)

Soap, Madam. Soap.

The Anatomy of the Horse

Near derelict. Neighbours – none.
Roof sound enough to keep out weather.
Trusses and purlins oak.
This will serve.

Tackle – bars pulleys slingdogs chains
well forged and paid for.
Good broad webbing.
Wind makes all creak like a Channel packet.

To begin at first light.

Draymen early.
Sun came up as full as an eye

and glazed   and shrank.

Moon like a pan of tallow.
1st mare slung up   rigged to the life.

To record laterally   from the front   from the rear.
Graphite & red chalk   pen & ink.

All to be done from nature.

Good breeze Thursday

new flensing knife
3 more buckets
twine

bone pit evening
ditch

cooperage Lincoln?

Mary   more clean rag for my face

Preparatory drawings 3rd Anatomical Table.
Fine facial nerves
blood vessels in red

Nature at every point surpasses art.
This I surmised as a child and confirmed in Italy.

Musculus caninus elevator of the corner of the mouth.

Lips patient   drooping

Have requested sound carcasses and would pay.
Draymen tipped out a spavined nag   galled

Rictus of laughter   'work for a dead horse'
musculus caninus

If certain muscles were to be disengaged would emotion be felt?

Seat of fear?
Suffering expressed in a tubercle.
The smooth hide has not suffered.

I will look into nature for myself and consult & copy her only.

Fiction of paradise – a stasis – a hell
joy without knowledge of suffering – folly

The godlike man?

Stuff out the great veins with quills.

No distaste in my mind.
What makes the gorge rise?

A man has discipline and can study.

Demonstrate what is.

Dreamed a foal in my Mary's belly.
She unmantled herself   brown robe falling

Caul of nerves web of veins
Foetus in its housing.
It wept.

Seat of the soul?

King cups over   cuckoos
Frogs in ditches   meadowsweet   dogroses
spires of loosestrife beginning to form

Rankness and sweetness

3rd carcass.
Flare of nostril turn of ear
& how the cropped tail moves

stars   viscous ivory

I have stamina and capacity.

5th Anatomical Table.
Flesh almost away.
Jawbone   moon   halved wafer

Remember how the mares squealed and bickered under the oaks.
Brush-tailed foals craning for the teat.

Work till the naked eye come at the naked truth.
When I have understood I shall paint them to the life.

Screaming of swifts   Larks pulleying up
Huzz and frenzy of messengers

I sluiced my head under the pump and put back my stained hat.

Wax to bulk out the concavities.

To reveal not judge

To represent those ligaments which bind down the tendons of the
muscles to keep them in their proper places.

Thundery this evening

Fetor   My palate clogged

What is the peritoneum enclosing the heavenly bodies?

Flygod sat whinnying on the orb of my eye
Mary waked me

Obverse of love – cruelty. Taste this.

My whetstone broken

I am weary   Eyes mere blebs

This muscle arising from the lateral part and ridge of the radius,
the thumb and forefinger of the horse being wanting, is inserted
into the imperfect metacarpal bone and lost in the ligaments in-
serted into that bone.
My thumb and forefinger balancing pencil and red chalk
abductor policis manus   extensor longus   brevis policis manus
moving

Broad ligaments of the eyelids fending off sleep

7th a black cob trampling air
& how that swings   ears laid back
rib cage enormous

belly hoist between the cranking limbs
& how that turns

I am Jonah   Diogenes in a barrel

Mary brought bread cheese & sweet water.
Feet set a little wide   Apron higher
She has reproached me not once

Preparatory drawings 18th Anatomical Table.

Summer at an end
my best knives honed almost away

Maps of flesh   charts of bone

Putrid carcass   creation of God
A Barbary horse which the lion took   ferocity of God
Mary at the water trough pounding my stiffened linen   tenderness
      of God

Interpret nothing.
Represent not love not hate but bone.

Head of femur lilac   beware lilac
Truth is as colourless as water

I understand no more than a waggoner

Hock pastern hoof   miring up sleep

Where does the life reside?

Study to engrave.

Remembrance

The Padre ministers to stumps of men.
At night the dreams come. God coughs
outside the tent, whinnies like a mule,
trails puttees of bloody bandages

and one day defects. *I am brought*
into so great trouble and misery
that I go mourning all the day long.

Three broad parishes, a small flock.
A fir-cone once plumb between the eyes
caused him to scream, a paper dart
caused a dark stain to spread.
– My text is taken from Isaiah
chapter forty-five verse fifteen. *Verily*
thou art a God that hidest thyself.

Dear children this cold November morning
and some of you I know are too young
yet, remember, many are called
but few chosen. Ponder Jeremiah:
The harvest is past, the summer is ended
and we are not saved. Verily
thou art a God that hidest thyself.

At the font, at the altar, he saw his face
quake in the eye of water the eye of wine.
Gave himself up. Tidied the musty hymnals
hung up his alb snipped off his ribbons,
at the vestry door courtmartialled himself
and fired the shot. Jackdaws in outrage
circled the tower a full two minutes.

We're staying at the Castlemount, Western Esplanade

I

When I am bored I climb the attic stairs
to visit Rosie in her wooden tent.
    The skylight is a stiff blue flag. There is
    the smell of varnish the smell of linen
    and the damp sweetish smell of wash-hand-stands
    arising from Rosie who is treadling.

Rosie is minder of a grand machine,
its figurehead a black and golden Sphinx.
   Just below the neck of the Sphinx there are
   two proud cones with gilded tips. Clothed ladies
   wear a single mound, right across, lower.
   Rosie has only the folds of her blouse.

She tilts her bentwood chair, her eyes blue chinks.
Give us a go please, Rosie, don't be mean!
   The substance of Rosie has shaken down
   into her boot which is dull black, a hoof
   with metal shanks hidden under her skirt.
   I think it is specially for treadling.

Be a good girl now, this won't pay the rent.
You pull this sheet and help me look for tears.
   A voice speaks from below. Rose? Rosie calls
   Yes Ma'am and says in a different tone
   Run along now there's a love; and I pause
   just to turn back into a public child,
   and march down. And that's Rosie for the day.

      II

Thinking he hears the children, Captain Kitto wakes
and shifts, and smiles; sighs in anticipation;
draws from his navy jacket chinking shells,
and waits; and sleeps again. His seamed cheeks
beneath the visor's curve are stained palm-green.
   Eyes on the canvas bulges, Annie steals
across the lawn's viridian deck, her breath
held like a captive petrel, till she peers
down at his freckled deepseasleeping head.
Under the sky's blue swell the few pale hairs
waver like seaworms. Close, her own head bowed,
she hears with glee the cowrie-clack of ancient teeth.

      III

Miss Bertram is teaching us how to paint the sea.
You need a sheet of good paper to take a wash,
a squirrel brush, few colours – blue, yellow, crimson –
and the water must be clean. Aim to work swiftly
and never, never to erase, or you'll forfeit
the quality of light, the vital quality.

The brush the sea uses is a shock of feathers,
something felted, a stick, a spar, a rag of weed.
Its colours are eelskin tarnish, rust, brown treacle.
It lays in the foreground temporary corals
of whiteling scum, and rubs out and rubs into holes
and works over and over and is never done.

IV

In sandy bathing suits, farther and farther
beyond the reach of voices.
                              In pictures,
rockpools appear like Japanese shells
flowering in a tumbler; but Annie and I
found grey barnacles, fawn jellies, black weed.

When we looked back, we saw that the undercliff
(where it is safer to play) was wearing
a huge concrete denture and holding
tiny red and blue people between its teeth.
They were jerking. We could not hear them cry.

V

Pink's the colour of what won't last.
There are pink celluloid dollies,
pink papier maché masks, balloons,
knickers with writing, candyfloss,
pink stick-on hearts, gobstoppers, rock –
everything struck pink and whirring
in the seaside wind.
                              Come along.
You don't want to waste your money.
You don't want to be buying those.

We sat down on the speckled sand,
stared at the waves and poked about.
Look! I've found somebody's jokebook!
You don't want to be reading that.
Are jokes pink? I'm no good at jokes
but I want to astound my friends.
Jokes are all about differences.
D'you think it's funny, the difference
between the seaside and the sea?

Christopher Pilling

ROY WILSON

CHRISTOPHER PILLING was born in Birmingham in 1936. He took a General Arts degree at Leeds, where he won the first New Poets Award with *Snakes and Girls* (Leeds University School of English Press, 1970). He has been a French teacher in Yorkshire and at Keswick School, from which he recently took early retirement. Other publications include *In all the spaces on all the lines* (Phoenix Pamphlet Poets, 1971) and poems in various anthologies, including *The Oxford Book of Verse in English Translation* (OUP, 1980). He has also translated editions of Corbière and Catullus. ●

ACKNOWLEDGEMENTS: *Adam's Dream, Anglo-Welsh Review, Critical Quarterly, New Poetry 2, New Welsh Review, Northern Drift* (Radio 3).

An affair with a chair

Why the wooden chair begins
walking towards me on its
four stilted legs
I shall never guess

Why tiny breezes blow
from its woodworm holes
each like a miniature slipstream
I shall never know

Why its bent wood back
leans forward to embrace
could-it-be-me I would love
to discover

And why it stumbles
just before it reaches
where I am sitting on its upright
sister I still need

to explain to my satisfaction

Webern

Dismissed as plink plonk. 'I can't stand
it. My head. I must go and lie down.'
You will only be able to see vertical
impressionisms flat on your back, eyes
up. Or closed. Aural heights scaled.
When I'm washing up I take it in
as linear and as patterned as my gestures
at the sink. Pause for the drips. Think
the crocks are musical (sic) clonk, clink.

Ophelia

was Elizabeth Siddal in a bath
under which oil lamps were kept burning.

Millais, absorbed in the folds
of her dress, did not see her turning

blue with cold. The lamps went out
unnoticed. Elizabeth froze.

Millais' gaze had been transfixed:
the bath was the stream,

the heat of his passion for the folds
Ophelia's madness,

both mixed, mixed, mixed as *idée fixe*,
unrequited until the hots and colds

of paints were one with Elizabeth
who, like Ophelia, was close to death.

The earth

You raise the creases
of the soles of your
feet to the scorch

you are just far enough
away from. Standing
on air, hiding your con

ventions, you lower
from me as you lean
in the air's hammock.

The sky takes your weight.
Your soles raise
a wizened grimace.

Encounter at the Post Office counter

I wanted a stamp for the parcel of figs
she put on the scales.
I'd wrapped them for Jill – they were straight from the twigs –
fresh as the milk in her pails.

As she worked out the cost her tresses were sprigs
of thrift, her breasts tiny whales.
I paid for the stamp for the parcel of figs
she'd put on the scales.

I looked up from my change. Gone was the wig,
gone was all thought of the mail.
She had blotted it out by assuming the rig
of…was it dragon or snake? Her tail
swished like milk in a bucket. A parcel of figs
lay ignored on the shelf. When the jigs
of my mind spelled a soft bed of nails
she'd fig-leaves for scales!

Dear Ez,

> *No one forgives you for what*
> > *you did, everyone forgives*

you for what you are. The loss
> to sanity is a spot
> > that's still sore though. Your word lives

on in *Lustra, A B C*
> *of Reading* and *Make It New,*
> > but not in your *foul-mouth* talk

from Rapallo. Let the plea
> of insanity stand; you
> > will then be released to walk

out of St Elizabeth's
> a free man, quite free to hate
> > all those who say you're *'batty'*,

anti-semitic, and death's
> too good for you. It's too late
> > though to disclaim the tatty

views that *dangerous fawning*
> J. White-is-Right Kasper *jerk*
> > – the thumb-nail is Hemingway's –

voices for you one morning
> when a Canto don't quite work
> > & you can't pin down forays

into wild substanceless thought...
> What advances do Sheri
> > and Marcella make you, you

who with *Bel Esprit* once fought
> for de-banking? A Merry
> > Christmas, Ez, and yes, what's new?

> Yours,
> > *Bull Carlos*

Specimen

My wife has left me. The child
            joins me now
and again for a half-day outing.
            We talk lessons.

History's a bore. The mistress
            says we have
to live the past over and over
            to distance

mistakes and make amends.
            We can't undo
any of it. Like the punishment
            she lashes out

if you turn round. Then there's
            geography.
I want to be where I am
            and like it.

I recognise the earth's crust
            but I forget
the name of the country I'm in
            and if the rivers

are specially long. Let's climb
            these boulders
and try and make the other side.
            It's better than Latin.

We're supposed to keep the verb
            till the end.
Apart from the roots, Latin's
            dead.
                        Are you cold?

The temperature of the blood
            changes to suit
external conditions. It's blowy
            in midstream.

H_2O is splashing our boots.
      Tormentil
on this grassy islet is small
      but brilliant:

for your buttonhole. If I hold
      your hand I can
reach that striated slate
      that must have been

carried down by the current.
      There's nothing
like it nearby. I can skim it
      to the other bank.

Let's go back now. Mother
      said I mustn't
be late for bed. The night
      falls quickly

at this latitude. I haven't told
      you I like
foreign languages. We study two.
      I'm quite fluent.

'Bye Dad.

Triptych
(in memory of my mother)

  I

Outside the hospital the sun lighted the leaves
of the low bushes. The lawns were trim
as Nurse and the beds she tucks, has tucked.

  II

Plastic knickers hang from the wall-cupboard
knob: they will dry quickly in spite of frills
in the stove heat. For wearing in the morning.

III

Fog is predicted. It has nothing to do
with death. Nor had that day at the end of April
when the bedclothes were drawn over her face.

You and you, in the pink
Matisse: Open window, Collioure 1906

Allow that the sea is pink, rich lobster pink,
a distinctly crustaceous pink. Allow it.
Let boats have orange masts, or madder red. Sit
way out over their side, aware that they may sink.
Sense that the sky is patchy, then note deft shades
of pastel seascape, horizontal streaks, dabs
of almost white, wavy blues, livid pink slabs
and leaning up against them, plunge your oar blades
into what you must know is bay. You won't see
that underneath each boat is a pane of blue
and glaze of bottle-green unless you're at the
open window in Collioure. Now can you be
sailing off down there *and* watching yourself through
a pink-framed window? Allowing you are you.

The Field

I stopped in the open under an apple bough,
with no tent but the dark, no pillow

but stooks – my Gallic itinerary crossed
by nightfall. I took my rest,

seeing stars between leaves. Sleep was slow
to come. A wind blew at the bole

of the tree, soughing. Leaves
replied. The stack came to life.

Mice tickled the straw with their patter:
the straw's teeth chittered.

Branched phantoms shook my head.
The sky, charcoal with cloud,

smouldered within. I slept.
My sleeping bag lay across France, wrapped

me from harm, the dawn journey to Ypres.
A light rain on my face woke me.

Fran

Her name is in the books I've bought at *Oxfam*:
There's an illustrated *Guide to Amsterdam*;
I, Jan Cremer, denizen of City Smut;
A Play of St George by a Poet Laureate;
a Narayan novel, published in Mysore,
bought in New Delhi, October '84:
The Vendor of Sweets; *Headhunters*, a pamphlet signed
by the poet, Keswick, 1979:
quite an odd collection. And I picked them out
almost as if my hand were guided – no doubt
I am a kindred spirit, but amassing
things she's grown away from – only past passing
fancies. What possessed her to give them away?
I squeeze them in my shelves – Fran is here to stay.

She lies silent . . .

She lies silent, her head in *The Plague*,
on the verge of sleep (verge is hardly the word
for this losing of consciousness, this vague
running of words before the eyes, a blurred
horde of rats on their final legs, muffled

squeaks in the far reaches of the mind
where there is no verge.) She is unruffled
by the tumours that solidify the rind
of silence, knowing deep within that she can lose
herself in reading or in sleep or in both at once
and the sanatorium of her marriage will use
her kindly, will tend each ugly protuberance
with a doctor's skill, with a nurse's oversight,
and, as a panacea, will put out the light.

Cast Away

*from a journal discovered on the Island of Ascension, offering
a full and exact relation of the author's being set on shore
by order of the commodore and captains of the Dutch fleet*

I

Useless to relate how I've strained my eyes –
often, misled by a distant sighting,
an earnest want of delivery will rise
in my shipshaped mind's eye, highlighting
my frenzy. The ceaseless wild ocean boom
intermixed with the sun's quite searing rays
presents to my senses a yellow gloom
like the moon when part obscured. When it stays
I expect to see in every streak and cloud
what I take to be a propitious sail...
Then dreadful the shock! And my cry out loud
as before my gaze the thing can fail
to materialise. What I see – no longer there –
has left within me the depths of despair.

II

The spring I found after weeks of searching
has run dry. I drink the blood of turtles.
I read my prayerbook constantly. Lurching
into recrimination, thought hurtles
off down unmade rock-strewn tracks. Voices drum
on my brain with every side-step. It's: 'You...

Bugger! Bugger!' hits hardest. Satan's come
for me – he's at my tent-flap with his crew,
banks on my dying of thirst. I must drink
my urine now. If only water would gush
from the rock as it did for Moses; ink
of the squid would be a godsend – and lush
green purslane meadows. That hullabaloo,
those shrieks, must be boobies to the rescue?

III

Having lived on birds' eggs,
birds shot with my fowling
piece, onions and rice,
I must bestir my legs
daily, the sun scowling
at me for my true vice
is unforgiveable,
I must find water and
the wherewithal to subsist.
If I'm thought liveable
I'll cross the burning sand,
my body will resist
hunger, thirst, but even
so, as a skeleton...

IV

Lust
for
man
has
sentenced
me
here.

Fear –
raw,
intense
as
can
be...

Dust...

Patricia Pogson

PATRICIA POGSON was born in Rosyth, Fife-shire in 1944. She trained as an art teacher, and has travelled and worked in India, Canada, and Australia. Publications include *Before the Road Show* (Rivelin Press, 1983), *Snakeskin, Belladonna* (Grand Piano, 1986) and *Rattling the Handle* (Littlewood Press, 1991). She has won prizes in national poetry competitions, and her work has appeared in anthologies. ●

ACKNOWLEDGEMENTS: Grand Piano, Rivelin and Littlewood Presses; *Ambit, Bête Noire, Between Comets, Kaleidoscope* (BBC Radio 4), *Lancaster Festival Anthology.*

Bee

Insects are neat in death,
do not bloat or stink.

This bee curled on a cucumber leaf
must have danced itself witless
against the indifferent glass.

Wasn't it Mandelstam
offered his love
a necklace of bees?

I wouldn't wear one.
Although they weigh
less than nothing,
feel strangely absent
held against the skin.

The double barbs on each foot
would catch.

I'd scratch my neck,
scatter bee dust.

A walking funeral.

Exits

A pair of clouded yellows
mating, back to back,
on an orange towel.

An hour later she took in
the washing, put it, folded
in the airing cupboard.

'Did those butterflies
leave?' he asked.
She rushed upstairs,
shook the towel.

They flew out, separately –
one through an upstairs window,
the other took the front door.

Face Mask

Inside the mask her eyes are very dark.
It is white, eggshell-hard, starting to crack.
Talking is out, and smiling; this chalk
has scribbled away her mouth, the track
where her lips meet is forbidden ground.
She hadn't intended to skim it over
her face, was looking for something when she found
the fat tube at the back of a drawer.
Was reminded of her mother, reclined
in an armchair, slices of cucumber
for eyes, hair scraped back, neck yellow, lined.
Her skin struggles for breath. She splashes water,
rubs through to the pink. Remembers how lost,
how naked she looked inside her white crust.

Going Home

This morning we escort Sharon,
who cannot talk.
Hugging her suitcase
she clumps to the back seat.
Her forearm is picked scabs,
knuckles misshapen.
When she left, the squawking
hurt our ears.
Nineteen, a bonny girl.
At her first period she screamed.
She strokes my hand, then her suitcase.
Her blunt moans speak pleasure.
The small hills make her ears pop –
that much I understand.
Her hands form flippers, penguin.
She swims to me. We laugh.
My shoulder aches from holding hands
across the seatback.

Resin

Rummaging a drawer I found the bee glue,
stuck to the bottom of an old perfume bottle.
Its clean smell had kept – resinous –
like nothing else…like all his presents:
peacock feathers, a Kangra print,
the thin pottery candle holder that sprang apart
in the post, and resisted my attempts
to stick it together. Black clay beads,
each stamped with a different pattern –
all buried somewhere about this room.

He liked me to watch him take the lid
carefully off the hive – his white gloves,
heavy veil, his delight like a bride's
with a chest of lavendered linen

as he lifted the combs. I expect
he still keeps bees, sings in the Bach choir,
has never learned to spell. I remember
how he would hum on journeys,
his neat rib-cage defining his shirt.
The waxy violet skin under his eyes.

Sleeper

Dear Steward, we're sorry we shock you like this
but you were so kind when we got on at Euston
– not everyone can cope with illness.
You'll find my husband's briefcase on
the rack near the window. The key's in
a blue envelope in my make-up case
(the zipped compartment). I think that's everything.
I suppose you think it's odd to go like this
but our neighbours are foreign, our only daughter
has small children, a husband's who's less
than useful. Please destroy this note before
we arrive. The police will deal with the rest.
The enclosed is for your trouble. As we both come
from Edinburgh, it seems like going home.

Hairdressing

Sifting fronds of your hair, she talks "style".
I twirl my black leatherette chair, watch
through a wing of mirror – your pale yellow
sweater resting in my lap. She says
the sun has leeched her customers away,
winter will be rich with tints, conditioners.
Draped in a polyester toga you are led off.
Chin up, head tilted back over a basin,
eyes loosely focussed on the ceiling, you drift
with the soapy fingers of a young assistant.

I go downstairs, leaf through racks
of Fiorucci jeans, think buying a pair
would spoil the pattern, try on a blouse.
Return to turbans, the stir of scissors –
damp curls hitting the floor, your pink face
humming from a beehive hair drier.
Jill the stylist has been betrayed;
her best friend dropped her for an actor.
The assistant picks up a dustpan, brush.
I see heavy grey curls inside your skull.

Amaryllis Belladonna

I cannot like you –
this sudden switch
from male to female;
that shrivelled foreskin
sloughed to reveal splayed buds.

Oscar would have sprayed
Attar of Roses on
your immaculate skirt,
changed the décor to match
your waxy extravagance.

Beardsley would have drawn
your attenuated stalk:
thin phallus whose wicked point
blossoms pink lilies
to sacrifice by candlelight...

and David Bowie would become you –
(the perfect deviant):
odourless, epicene,
tinted exotic
on a hollow stick.

In Dreams

When they ask us to visualise
I try to make my box three dimensional,
to distinguish between four kinds of flowers
or feel the golden liquid flow along my spine,
but there's nothing really, only my shuddery breath,
fingers tensing, tongue glued to the roof of my mouth.

The doctor says I should write myself a letter,
get you out of my system. I told him exorcism
is for ghosts. Strangely, he's not interested
in my dreams, even though one of them recurs
each month before my period. The same room
with the open fire, each coal picked out in gold,

a stone sink in one corner, the cold tap
dripping into the bowl of a teaspoon, the child
hidden behind a chair. You're about somewhere,
the girl is yours. Why is she terrified of you?
I go to comfort her but always wake up
pain-clenched, thighs sticky. Check with one finger,

make a red print on the white wall. I know
if I could stir it into your coffee the pain would make
an unbreakable seal. The nurse who sponges the wall
says I'd be good for the ducking stool if this wasn't
England, the twentieth century. Who cares;
I'm in the coven of crazy women.

The other dream is of home. It's April,
just before the rainy season. I'm four years old.
As my father carries me on his shoulders through
the flower market, each stall holder hands me a bloom;
jasmine, lotus, frangipani, and my favourite –
the white bell from the temple tree.

Waking I smell garlands, coriander leaves,
have to drag my senses across continents
to this long pale box, one geranium
turning its stiff face to the wall.

Fifteen

I was helping my mother
spread mattresses on the verandah
when you came to introduce yourself –
our new landlord, from the flat upstairs.

Your cook offered us a tray of rice each day
and gave my little brother biscuits.
My father replied with lemons from our tree,
green mangoes for chutney.

Sometimes I'd soak my sari in iced water
and cycle for miles, burned down
to six stones in as many weeks.
My father took me to the doctor.

Or carry a mat down to the beach,
sit and wait for the sun to come up;
pretending to meditate.
Ebony fishermen dragged their nets ashore.

Once we swam at sunset in luminous water,
walked the dunes while our clothes dried;
my choli stiff with salt as I tugged to loosen
the fused knot in my petticoat string.

You tried to lift me over a sand bar
but I resisted. Offered to drive me
to Binsar, the valley of flowers.
But my father sent you a letter,

took me to my aunt in Bombay
who started the search for a suitable husband:
a good boy whose horoscope
would echo mine.

Apples

You phone to say birds have gouged
your apples, wasps scoured the flesh –
left skins limp on the ground.

So you've picked them less than ripe,
peeled them with the black-handled knife
that's wasp-waisted from too much sharpening.

Your own skin has been eaten thin by steroids,
will bruise at the slightest knock,
breaks if caught awkwardly.

Sometimes when I ring your voice
is shingle sucked over cold sand.
I can hear your lungs.

Bruising, exhaustion, nights propped on pillows,
hours sweating over menthol when no doctor came.
Subject taboo, my sisters tell me.

'You still there?' Your voice
cuts the thoughts tumbling through my head.
'We've still a few left –

would you like a crumble?'

Peter Rafferty

PETER RAFFERTY was born in Carlisle in 1952. He took a degree in Geography at Manchester, and did research in Geomorphology at Durham. Currently he works as manager of a betting shop, is a part-time wine importer, and full-time Italophile. ●

Back End

Another summer we must have blinked and missed
as iron enters the soul of dews
and trees announce their redundancies,
while the first leaves shuffle, disconsolate in doorways.

The crack swirls, as thick and familiar
as them, or betting shop smoke:
'A poor year, aye, nae doot aboot that,'
'There's nivver been twa good days togither,'
'A good fortneet in April, and that was the lot.'
And if all are agreed things aren't what they were,
they stopped looking for reasons in June.
Resignation's sunk in – the old candidates for blame,
say like Concorde, and all them Russian missiles,
are by now all but forgotten.
Some still raise hopes: 'We'd a good September last year
and it's been nice down South and all,'
though privately, their thoughts are for sun in Spain,
or have given the job up – well, next year could be better:
Yes, there's always next year...

                                    For however clapped out,
with wings rusted, shot gaskets, this once-good earth can seem,
there's always the hope it can be patched up,
of renewal. The thought just might keep us sane:
It's as if it were drawn at the top of our slates,
etched into the intellect before evidence of sense,
a part of the framework, with space and time,
preconditioning all we see,
till it's always with us, built into our tales
of Persephone's release, the Resurrection,
Barbarossa and Arthur, asleep in their caves,
awaiting the call to make their countries whole.

Yet perhaps it's too lulling – shops rise up, neon-bright
from the braziers and rubble,
while grass grows to shrubs, and shrubs to trees
in kestrel-patrolled motorway cuttings.
When last year's quarries become the next nature reserves,
the irrevocable becomes hard to credit,
while we keep on hoping it will all work out,
all be given back somehow.
So too with biographies – the subjects' deaths
become as hard to believe in as our own,
and you think that, almost, they might be living still,
if Beethoven had only had better doctors;
if only Wordsworth hadn't caught that chill.

If only we hadn't cut down the rainforests;
If only we hadn't slaughtered all the whales…

View from the Bathysphere

Things swim
in
and out of focus:

so many dazzling fish

so much forking, right angling of shoals:

pictures flashed
in the flip between channels,
distant chatter, as you pick up the phone.

Sometimes, we lower ourselves into the water;
in remembering, forget,
lying in the warm buoyancy.
Re-emerging, air slaps coldly on the skin.

But at others, uncalled,
from dark pressure
phosphorescence
can rise, goggle-eyed
Medusa, a face

we cannot bear to look on.

After Carnival

Je suis la Gondole enfant chérie
Qui arrive a la fin de la fête.
            LAFORGUE

The doors swing out, and spill you down the stair,
glass still in hand – how you have laughed tonight!
You reel on still, and scorn the ermined glare
of *grandi* from the old Republic's might.

Ah, they and the dark are easily outfaced
on landings bright with masks of sun and moon,
and Harlequin. Your gondolier has paced
the quay, he too now tricked as Pantaloon.

…Opening the cover – you must have dozed,
her head for a while slumped on your chest –
fog catches the throat, water-sway reimposed;
sunken stone scrapes as the keel comes to rest.

You look round. 'But these aren't our mooring posts…
This is not Palazzo…' 'There is no mistake.
You are called to this house of seven ghosts:
of one drowned, and six who'd have that he break

his fast. It is yours.' And you see the festoon
of weights and chains round him. Lanterns falter,
blink out – to snow plumes, the wide grey lagoon,
as light pales, falling like a tired bird to its water.

66°7'N / 22°17'W
(Kaldalon, NW Iceland)

And I have stepped into the iceworld – at the snout
where stonefalls punch each hour,
burning plunge-pools into the crust, that greys
with wind-blown flies and rock flour;
where mudflows dribble across the snowbanks
from perched lateral moraines,
and meltwaters rumble beneath the feet
like distant underground trains.

But is this no more than paddling in the surf
as Atlantic rollers bore in?
The chirp of snow buntings drifts here still;
downvalley, sheep graze; a racket of terns
snaps at the head by the fjord.
And something at least can be understood,
considering, by these glacier eaves,
esker and mountainfall,
but beyond the slump of bergs from the iceshelf,
the last ogives, blue foliations,
past the nunataks' thrust,
black-splintered rocks,
no refuge even for lichens,
is the final placelessness,
white of the inlandsis,
and its low interrogative sun:
heatless, cheerless as the bulb in a cell,
yet melting the sky to the horizon.
Six months of night drain the winds of a world
to a black sump that traps them
to spin tatterdemalion
and aimless as the banner of the Futile.

Sense numbs there. How sense, beneath the feet,
the compaction of faded footprints?
Or how the processes at the base
of granite, three hundred atmospheres,
five million years of snow,
still have singularity's zero sum
of stasis, absolute as that of Cocytus,
and the crushed blooms of a spring that never came?

Note: 'Singularity' is here used in the restricted sense of a point at which
physical laws cease to be meaningful, the terms reducing to zero or infinity.

Willowherb

The counter's crackle piles up the digits
as dragon-tooth-spawn, or blown in on the wind,
lumpen foxgloves spring thick as gold-rush tents
in shanty towns, where we have slashed and burned.

Aboriginal, the first colonists in ruin,
they are honoured by being bulldozed from the site
by plainly more civilised, fastidious species,
their rights dating at the least to Constantine,

and are packed off, to mark time, on their reservations,
to scratch for a living, among the dust and ash,
while the rest of the world, with sharpened scythes,
riots mercilessly to its climax.

Off the Beaten Track

Automotrici stutter along the branch lines
of the plain, where the folds of the first Appennines
twist to knots that faith only unpicks through the haze
above little halts, sunk among crickets and maize;

where the soft clack of sandals on cloister flags
has slowed to a shuffle, now candlesmoke drags

a screen across canvases, dark as the veil
of a widow who numbers her beads by the rail.

There, best in the world, is where I would stay,
a village Capo di Stazione,
with my gold-braided cardinal cap, that would greet
the two-hourly trains, hear them fade through the heat.

And I would have too a little plot under vine
I'd drive to in evenings, then when the new wine
was ready, a well-picked few would come round,
tilt the year in the glass, its sunlight unbound.

In the Madonna Dell' Orto

We have our moments.

It's like putting your hundred lire in,
in a side chapel, in late afternoon,
to cast shadows from the altar columns,
and light on the restored Bellini
strikes blue in the Madonna's veil.

Then the meter clicks off,
and we are left, eyes blinking,
trying again to get used to the darkness,
to retrace the lines of the Child's benediction,

The Virgin's look of love.

Personal
(after Carlo Felice Colucci's 'Personale')

Tireder than usual I got up
how the heatwave weighs us down
with stilted movements I shaved
like some makeshift automaton
and how many times will that be, how many

the unleavened tally of days
dryly, 'how many times',
the priest would ask, in a hiss
he makes no tale of the giving and having
from courtesy's gifts you do not turn ungracious
one heart stopping while another fibrillates
nor ever will I hear absolution's brass band
with its touch of black hangings, its touch
of the negroes of Nashville, no never
to make up, I possess some fine aftershaves
minor blackmails – I know of whom
some small tufts too for the liturgy
of well-intentioned beneath-the-arms shaving
and now and again I try them all on the skin
one after the other, observantly,
chance companions that jog briefly back to life
so I too can return just a bit to the clownish
now that follies are tailing away,
I seek out, I study, I interpret the droll baldness
a Sibyl's two-edged prophecies
and shiver as if I had long been waiting
for someone come from long exile, arriving
on a special, strictly personal flight
or as if duties pressed me, who knows for whom
in those jovial freemasonries
the others, happy hostages all, by the sea
so far from the frozen silences
and ice-floes of the Lapps
a word, a dried fish, one never knows
old love, one still does not know
we hermit crabs in search of shells
and in the age-long pause I take count of the scuffling
a sharpness of staring,
strange vibrations revolve
polish facings
to the equal of the day,
the oval glass like the Madonna's face
the blind image in the square frame
may remain and not surrender
between dusty light
and this aftershave threnody
from a dreamer to the shadows

whom the clock looks over
the ancient meridian intact still
after all,
and just about punctual, makes for the door
every morning, if still living

Passage
(after Carlo Felice Colucci's 'Passaggio')

Of boats, of boats
I would talk to you
with all flags flung upon the wind
in yellow of quarantine
in his soft cap upright on the prow
my father
at his century
pointing the way
without tolls
the waiting dreadful even so,
a peaceful passage it would have been
for us incredulous
at flimsy sails
pages torn from textbooks
hands raised in uncertain
gesture of farewell
or the dried geraniums
from ancient banisters
flower of truce
on a grocer's sign
in the window
the small sad tale,
now it is the sin of Adam
that I unfold to you

Ben Scammell

BEN SCAMMELL was born in Bristol in 1966 and moved to Cumbria when he was nine, where he attended Cockermouth and Keswick schools. He has a degree in English and Philosophy from Bristol University, and works at odd jobs in between his writing. ●

From the Provinces

The train is right on time,
like a god pulling into the station.

It might as well be full of candles
that pale the faces

staring out the frosty window
before setting off again

for the bleak snows of Leningrad.
The huge fur coats from behind

look like bears to wave them off
and from the front

you can see a talc of snow
scatter unearthly gazes.

The Party

She was a brazen package of smoulder
and red nails, hair
combed to the point of let-down.

Even her distraught manner was distraught
and visibly in conference with
some interior pain, local –

I did not ask why.

An actor speaks

I am the used-arrow collector
in second-rate films,
scampering across a drawbridge of few words.
Sometimes the camera crew disappears
and the characters, the kings and queens,
look at me, and see I am wearing costume too,
and I answer with funny words. Once I saw
Elizabeth Taylor dressed up as *La Reine*
looking a right noodle.

Now the lighting man and sound engineer
have gone, the scenery is packed away;
I wait for a famous actor to take me
into the wings and offer advice
on drinking clinics, how to be personable
and generate friends, elusive when needed.

I will not be interviewed, that is certain.
I have no need of interviews. They bore me
and I want nothing to do with them.

The latest is that I have been offered
a new part in a science-fiction series.
Perhaps one day I will graduate
to picking up bullets in the Second World War.

Working for British Telecom
(for Emma Vaughan)

You were framed by your dark chestnut hair
    in a white landscape of arms and wrists,
    your pulse slowed to a sleeping Buddha;
    vague romantic relations
    you find in all the travel books.
    On certain days, the nights would become
    a way in to personalities not unlike our own;
    a mimicry of the best intentions.

On that first day I couldn't make
    head or tail of the nightingale
    that called you up out of thin air,
    making you into the girl next door.
    I manned the telephones
    and learned how your father committed suicide.
    I too had problems, therefore we

talked of families and how they've gallivanted through
    more devils and downtown blues
    than days could bat eyelids at.
    If not quite heaven

at least there were conclusions to be drawn
    as Christmas neared in chocolate
    and tangerines, adding a vivid spark to life;
    awareness that the building we worked in
    repeated its ground floors to the top,
    and of politics; bowling under-arm
    at the blue-rinsed shires, how it is easy
    to mistake a lone robin for the invasion.
    The water only came up to our knees.

But talk of misery-guts soon evaporated,
    leaving us at home on our desks, sticking
    to the scripts, or else we would be out
    on our ear. The days became longer,
    stretched, and turned into weeks.
    And if clichéd, it was true:
    tender was the night, on certain days.

For a Six Year Old

He is learning at a rate of knots
   how to tie his own shoe-laces;
   at that tender age when no-one
   can accuse him
   of sticking his nose
   into other people's business.

In other words, he is
   hermetically sealed
   against the outside world.
   He has not yet had to encounter
   a problematic social life,
   or jump off at the deep end.

The seasons have barely formed
   in his small head. But when they do
   there will be no idleness, no going back.

For the time being he misses
   what goes on around him.
   He is unaware that children
   have been written about before;

or that the Christmas lights have failed
here, here, and here.

Diaries
(for Sally, Lucy, Sarah and Michelle)

I had been trying to get through all day.
   The lines must have been down
     over Stoke or Bayswater

when the mist cleared
   and the landscape resumed
     its assault on the horizon.

Making light of wind and rain
    I put on my boots and step down
        to the bottom of the garden,

full of Chinese watercress.
    (My diary open where the staples glint through.)
        Someone has got to fetch the coal

feed the dogs, etc. All this goes on
    like the interminable search for a girlfriend;
        the sifting of books, people and parties.

As often as not I am
    headed in that direction, presumed
        innocent until sherried under mistletoe

where I listen
    to the hoary munificence
        of elected speakers;

the girl with the bloke round her arm.
    Frost and sunlight that evaporate
        to lightning and thunder

the next morning, loose change
    recovered at the traffic-lights
        from inside pockets.

And meanwhile I watch the puddles glitter,
    knowing how long their journey is
        from the underworld, and wary

of the entrances to caves.
    In case I get stung
        I carry a dock-leaf

and a dry patter about the after-life.
    In the evening I go to see friends,
        knocking on doors when no one's in.

More Rain
(for Graeme, Jim and Lil)

A day perched at ground-level –
    cloud-cuckoo land for worms
    and other members of the species,
    face-down in the landscape of families –

a writing no-one cares to read.
    Only the prickly spines of the hedge-hog
    that has blown a tyre in the back garden
    makes requisite reading for the time of year:

the seasons in their menopause.

Now is the time that you have to die laughing
    as you learn to fall over again, or at least
    be able to spot the nudge and wink
    of small animals in hibernation...

the fuzzy stain of the bonfire
    and a cloud of ants that needle the crotch.
    And the New Year, which comes through
    a small gap in the branches –

high-points for the meteorologist.
    This weather, adamant in the rain-season,
    could be likened to the old-boy network
    of shrinking ties, a shirt size

whisked to fahrenheit in the time it takes
    to wish a kindly brother
    well down the quiet back-roads of France.

Sin

Who asks forgiveness
but sends his mouth to the job
like a baker his son
like a country its soldier.

Stranger to a small child

A friend of my father came to stay
and went away

wishing he could find
a point in space
from which to lever
the world away from its pain.

My Lost Brother

And last but not least, my own brother –
who has made, out of petrol and hormones,

a little world for himself, a paradise
of hang-gliders and cars;

where he is clearly recognisable
as himself,

swung in mid-air
above a hill-side.

He has gone to Switzerland
to take in the sights

working his way back
through his own hard-won youth,

its easy roundabouts and hard spring ground;
his world rolled tight as a sleeping-bag.

William Scammell

ACKNOWLEDGEMENTS: Peterloo
Poets, for poems from William
Scammell's collections.

WILLIAM SCAMMELL is the author of four
books of poems, *Yes and No* (1979), *A Second
Life* (1982), *Jouissance* (1985), *Eldorado*
(1987), all published by Peterloo Poets, and
a critical study of *Keith Douglas* (Faber,
1988). He received a Cholmondeley Award
in 1980, has won awards from the Arts Coun-
cil and Northern Arts, and in 1989 won the
Poetry Society's National Poetry Competi-
tion. He is currently a part-time lecturer in
English in Newcastle University's Continuing
Education Department, Writer in Residence
at Nottingham Polytechnic, and a Selector
for the Poetry Book Society. He writes regu-
larly for the *Times Literary Supplement*,
Spectator, *London Magazine*, *Poetry
Review*, and other journals. Forthcoming
publications include two new books of
poems, an anthology of nature poems, and a
selection of Ted Hughes's critical prose. ●

St Bees in Winter

The kids shoot out of the car roaring
to meet their maker – instantly attuned
to that huge battery and assault. High tide,
high winds, shriek at the gaping shore;
they shriek right back, like pebbles
flung back and forth in the sling of surf.
One picks at daisy chains of foam;
the next is hooting back the ebb; then all,
mad as bullfighters, are down the sea's throat,
dwarfed by the breakers' thundering rush.
Wet feet, wet legs, wet bouncing bottoms...
I swear if we loosed the rein of our eyes
they'd be out of this world in minutes,
tumbled through to the sinners and saints
gunning their ghostly spray at our white lips.

Christmas at Bristol

'To behold the death of a child – it is a suffering beyond conception' – SARA COLERIDGE
'Little lamb! & the snow would not melt on his limbs!' – S.T. COLERIDGE

The baby coughed and coughed, clearing its lungs
as of some monstrous hook let down by God.
Sam iced fast in Germany – *Es ist zwar*
ein recht gutes Bier; Wm and Dorothy
not to be found, anonymously siring
the Lucy poems. Ice packed the Elbe,
coldest winter for a hundred years. At one
Sun Feb 10, Berkeley convulsed and died.

Soldiers are blown up or run frenziedly
at death, lust beaming them through
darkness. The old are slowly dragged
past the highest wave. Only the strong
joy of Wm sings total eclipse.
Sara lived it, vein by vein,
hands plucking out the gelid eyes of hope.
Through life she kept the dead birthday.

God is conceived in those High Renaissance
and virgin mothers: they are the rock
on which love hammers and is shod.
To give birth and see the branch sapless
or hacked down – it is a suffering
beyond conception. All light is humbled;
blind snow-glare of the father and the son.

The Screes

The screes are speeding down at perfect pitch
before they tuck themselves in silences
Wastwater seals and never means to post.
Clouds snuffle by, fat bridesmaids plump with tears.

The screes are swarming up the cliff to lay
their case in heaven. The water's indigo.
A cormorant, wings unpacked, hung out to dry,
stands phoenix-fixed upon a rock. The screes

are drowning out upon the lake, face up.
It rains stops rains; somewhere a bark. The screes
are deep and thinking one emotion through

like Hegel's avalanche of counterpoint
prodding the Absolute to a day's turn.
Sheep press their starter buttons all night long.

Jean Rhys

Your dresses never kept you warm.
Your dancing seldom kept you fed.
A worse insolence than the waiters'
bowed to right and left. In bed

where most things start and end, you wept
and drank too much (the traveller's rest)
and sank the last two fingers for
the fragrant islands of the past.

Cheap music costs, cheap feelings lie.
Both are good to have. The man
who's got to take the record off
will put the record on again.

They called your number just too late.
You missed the boat, you fluffed the show.
Put your immortal stockings on...
Chin up, and cheerio.

Holiday Inn®

Retrospective

Gwen John's women only just
make it onto the canvas. Pale blue's
the colour of the birth they choose
not to announce. They're fading fast

into a future of unreachable
addresses, high single bed,
cats, letters posted or unposted,
three or four cowslips on the table

murmuring of Ophelia's trailed coat,
one fork and spoon, devoutly crossed,
some sort of mirror, spotted with rust,
a knife-edged cameo at the throat.

Any minute now the master
will come hurrying in from the storm
with the tablets smoking under his arm –
the ultimate disaster.

Eclogue: Clerk of the Weather
(for Pamela Woof)

> *If solitude, or fear, or pain, or grief,*
> *Should be thy portion…*   ('Tintern Abbey')

A.   The nut-brown maid of Grasmere plays
     amanuensis to the lays
     of William and the weather, which,
     entire unto itself, is rich
     in characters, and scenes, and plots,
     monumental rorschach blots
     streaming over Helm Crag, bowed
     in great long paragraphs of cloud
     or sounding quiet midnight's noon
     with all the quarters of the moon.

B.   Aye, Dorothy, poor lass. Was her
     twinned up a poet's character,
     two poets, mebbe. Then she fell
     back on the thinkin' of hersel
     and Lord knows but the weather turned.
     Naebiddy knows what she learned –
     days and nights as strange to her
     as to the fust Mrs Rochester.
     Up in her room she twitched, she crowed
     like some old gipsy on the road.

A.   *The moonlight lay upon the hills –*

B.   *– like snaw.* Aye. Pretty stuff.
     It sells the beuks, and's true enough.
     But what came down in her distress?
     *My own thoughts are a wilderness
         not pierceable by any power.
     I have fought and fretted and striven –
         and am here beside the fire.*
     Where once all nature was lawgiver
     she sees the *naked seed-pods shiver.*

A.   Jean-Jacques, maybe, was not so clever
     in banishing the Fall? For they
     lacked reasons for mortality
     and fallings-off, and said so in
     great heartfelt bursts of poetry
     which found scant room for death or sin
     in Grasmere's tolerable Eden.

B.   William was God, and mebbe too
     he was the serpent.

A.   Incest?

B.   Pooh!
     But love – love is its own taboo,
     festering slowly on the stem.
     The naked seed-pods: what of them?
     You'd think in getting down the shrill
     raw beauty of a daffodil
     they'd said it once and once for all…

A.   Nay. Lucy played in sun and shower –

B.   He struck her dead, made death a flower
     that splits the rocks. Remember when
     they laid down in their graves an hour
     and went together home again?
     She died, in life, for love. Just that
     sings through her brief magnificat.
     One note she held, like that last leaf
     she speaks of, pure atomic grief
     that whirls and spins perpetually
     in the gaunt socket of the tree.

A.   If they'd had modern drugs –

B.   Aye, give
     or take an epoch, she might live
     as we do, and have dosed her heart
     with the black drop of modern art;
     conned the dream that she was in
     and smote it with an aspirin...

A.   We love a mystery – such bliss
     in tortuous analysis!
     But there's no need. She aged, and fell
     into disease. She grew unwell.

B.   Unsomething, aye: unhinged, unmanned,
     nor never wore a wedding band
     again. *News – I must seek for news*
     she says. There is none. She is bruised
     to silence, soon to pass on down
     to her dear Godchild, *one green gown.*

A.   *A mind o'erthrown –*

B.   *Is Babylon*
     in ruins. And we know no more
     than that affecting metaphor.
     The wild lights in her eyes died down
     to solitude, and fear, and pain
     within a babby's bonnet pent.
     The Wye ran on, magnificent,
     unchanging. All the words were spent
     and bought her a last quiet place
     to know the Bedlam of her face,
     fronting the worst that time had done
     and all the elements, but one.

Inventions
(i.m. Norman Nicholson, 1914-1987)

I

There are lakes in our region
        small English lakes
with even smaller islands floating in them
        holding a dark stand of trees.

Only the very luckiest roots
        get taken on there.

II

All down the coast old factories
        revert to soil and scrub.
It doesn't take much to heave off
        raw industrial brick.
But these old trees are tough. They bow
        to no one but themselves.

III

Water hammers on the beach,
        dimples in the lake,
it holds up its dress this way
        and that way in the beck.

There floats the island
        which is a fist of earth
or an invention of the mind.

Just one step, it says,
        just one more step
and either the world will open
        or it will have dodged back
into your pocket, like a coin.

IV

I was late for your funeral, Norman.

The wind blew against me, the car
    slowed, three Herdwicks skittered
on the narrow Thirlmere road.
    It seemed to take forever to get round
and round to your spit of land.

I came back by the coast, under Black Combe,
    thus making of it a round trip.
The June fields grew a yellowish grass,
    that shade old Faber covers
fade to, when a book was a real book.

Nicola
(for Tim and Liz)

In eighteen months she has grown
to fit her rompers – perfectly.
The soft hair too has started
on its journey down her back.
When it's two feet long
she will have a small museum
of Lilliputian china in her room
and O Levels for every three inches.
Meanwhile she is all-coloured and ignorant,
padded up against damage in transit,
shoving a giant head up close
against the bending cheekbone
of her mother's smile.

And all this in The Nab
where Quince and Hartley dreamt of fame,
eating the young pink char from Rydal,
learning first how hard it was
just to wake up to the light on the lake.

Trains

1
If ever there was a vehicle for nostalgia
2
Puffing along between heaven and earth
3
There is the carriage of childhood
4
The interview that will dig up your days
5
No such thing as an undecided train
6
Throbbing and slowing. Full tilt. Inch by inch
7
Ears eyes nose hands tongue
8
There is terror of stepping on the wrong train
9
Terror of stepping on the only train

One Man

A block of flats, somewhere in Turin.
A stairwell, neither here nor there, anonymous
as scuff-marks   wrappers   buttons   echoes.
It is the spiral steps are mounted in
with iron uprights, shabby at the knees,
a rail to haul on, bleak infinities

of doors and doorways, opened just a crack.
Warm air blurts out, to tangle in the hall
with blasts of cold. It sees a body fall

through bony floors, then spider on its back.
The telex throbs, spitting its letters home.
Implacable chatter at the gates of Rome.

Primo Levi's dead. One man has gone
back down alone, to circle endless fire.
Stigmata of pure reason and barbed wire,
whose corpus is the earth he walked upon,
receive, bind, mortify this blessed ghost,
laid down among the shadows he engrossed.

Some lines of Dante haunted him, compounded by
tormenting gaps. The dull cadavers sang
in broken words, while mothers deftly hung
out children's clothing on the wire to dry.
It flaps there still, the only way it can.
Clean air blows through it, moving like a tongue.

The Walk
(for Jan)

This is as far from home as you can get,
back-of-Skiddaw's unspectacular fells
in the much-mapped, massively-written-about
walker's heaven of lark-sprung heathery hills

and falls. Dash Falls, for instance, doing away
with itself with revolutionary vigour.
And though he's long been lost to the light of day
you can still make out where that stooping, peaty figure

nicked and shovelled a small dark cliff of earth
some yards above the beck, backed up the horse,
took in the giant folio of the heath
and carried it off to long-lost Skiddaw House.

It's all but derelict now, the grove of larch
thrown down, in some old tempest, like t'ai chi,
root-tables torn aloft, pegged out to watch
a shower pass, the needles' slow decay.

Squat on a trunk, take in the broken star
of household glass, the stone shed on its back,
the soft, complicit turf, a clattery pair
of wingbeats, turning the silence in its lock.

Poem for a Younger Son

This one steps into an outsize pair of wings
and commits hubris that he lives to tell.
One minute a model of Epstein's rock drill,
padded and helmeted, the next he flings
his torso off the face of the fell

into strong creaky arms of wind
that dandles him up like a baby. There
all earth recedes to a miniature
of unperspectived, geometric land
and only the cloud-base sings in his ear.

I'm left behind, with an upturned face
and lurching heart, as he skates on air
then turns and mounts up, higher and higher,
waving (damn fool!) from the height of his bliss,
whirled out like the topmost spark of a fire.

And the blaze is kindled by all his years
as a last-born, follower, third man on the rope
oppressed by the company he must keep:
the oxygen of a mother's fears,
and father's rules, a tape with a loop.

No sage, no art-encrusted connoisseur
saw the Lakes like this; nor you and me.
The poet trusts only to metaphor
but the poet's son knows how to fly,
what inspiration is really for,

the code of the competent: lightly keep
skimming the silence, smile into your beer.
Words for the wordy, parsons for sheep,
and the rush of the angel nowhere, nowhere
but waking out of the family sleep.

David Scott

MOIRA CONWAY

ACKNOWLEDGEMENTS: David Scott:
A Quiet Gathering and *Playing
for England* (both Bloodaxe).

DAVID SCOTT was born in 1947 in Cambridge. From 1980 to 1991 he was vicar of Torpenhow and Allhallows in west Cumbria, and has recently moved to Winchester. He won the *Sunday Times*/BBC national poetry competition in 1978 with the poem 'Kirkwall Auction Mart'. His first book of poems, *A Quiet Gathering* (Bloodaxe Books, 1984), won the Geoffrey Faber Memorial Prize, and his second, *Playing for England* (Bloodaxe Books, 1989), was a Poetry Book Society Recommendation. *How Does It Feel?*, a book of his poems for children, was published by Blackie in 1989. He is also co-author of several successful children's musicals for stage and television, including *Captain Stirrick* (1981), *Bendigo Boswell* (1983), *Jack Spratt VC* (1986) and *Les Petits Rats* (1988). ●

Scattering Ashes

The nose of the pick-up lifted
into the sky and then down onto the fell
as we made our way to the spot
he drove to himself to drop hay
in bad winters and as he got lame.
From where we stopped, we could see
the farm house and the tops of hills
which for a moment seemed to pour in
on the random heap of an old sheep pen.
Willy fed the ash out like a trail
of gunpowder. It blew among us
taking our words with it: ashes; sacred;
our brother here departed. We stood
fixed awkwardly as hawthorn trees watching
the white ashes of a man who once stamped
this ground, fly off in fancy with the wind.
Arms were wrapped like scarves round shoulders;
and the dog, whistled out of the back,
wove in front of the car a sad reel
as we followed the fresh tracks home
through all the open gates on the land.

Kirkwall Auction Mart

There are no bolts that do not exactly
fit the gates into and out of the store-ring.
Hundreds of times a day the same slamming iron
marshals cattle lots, hooves fighting the sand,
until the stick smacks them into view.
A nod decides the hidden bidders
and for these ghosts a litany is sung
bridging the jump in bids by the ancient
rattling of tongues until a bashed hand settles it.
Paper slips locate the buyers. We might
have guessed it would be a man of dull cloth,
hunched over the front rail, his smoke
joining the wreath of snorted breath high up
in the roof, who knew his business, and bought.

Flanking Sheep in Mosedale

All summer the sheep were strewn like crumbs
across the fell, until the bracken turned brittle
and it was time they were gathered
into the green patchwork of closer fields.
Dogs and men sweep a whole hillside in minutes
save for the stray, scared into a scramble
up a gully. A dog is detached: whistled off
by the shepherd who in one hand
holds a pup straining at the baling twine
and in the other, a crook light as a baton.
His call cuts the wind across the tarn:
it is the voice of the first man, who
booted it across this patch to bring
strays to the place where he would have them.
You can tell that here is neither love nor money
but the old game fathers have taught sons to win.
It is done well, when the dogs
lie panting, and the sheep encircled dare not move.

Letters from Baron Von Hügel to a Niece

His day was not really complete until
he sealed with a gentle middle finger
a letter to his niece, heralding the arrival
of books. It smelt of camphor. The advice
was a comfort to her: 'Give up Evensong,
and even if dying never strain.'
It was surprising counsel from one so scrupulous;
whose sharp pencil noted on both margins of a page,
and hovered, like a teacher's, over spelling.
Walking into Kensington with the letter,
his muffler tight against the frost,
he reassures himself that directing a soul
is not only a matter of angel's talk, it is
also the knack of catching the evening post.

Winston Churchill

On the morning of the funeral,
when the cranes were practising their salute,
the Myth woke up to his last responsibility.
He elbowed his way into his braces,
each shoulder some sort of clinched strategy,
and the trousers settled like theatre curtains
over the last generation of shiny shoes.

The responsibility lay around
our semi in the form of symbols
just a bit too big to manage:
the British Warm that gave me aircraft-carrier
shoulders; five inches of measly bath water;
and a rhetoric, which my father could turn on
for the small fee of being believed.

Illness

Hers was the vacant seat by the door.
To choose the nearest was her way of coping
with the recent bother of always feeling tired,
especially today, with the sudden change in weather.
At first, the shopping basket held her up,
but sleep soon capsized her
to the angle a holed tanker is towed at.
I wondered if the illness would come as a surprise
to her, leaving the family to shop for muddled meals;
and how she would wake up eventually;
by a kindly tap at the end of the line,
or in panic, not sure of the stop.

Locking the Church

It takes two hands to turn the key
of the church door, and on its stiffest days
needs a piece of iron to work it like a capstan.
I know the key's weight in the hand
the day begins and ends with it.
Tonight the sky is wide open
and locking the church is a walk
between the yews and a field of stars.
The moon is the one I have known
on those first nights away from home.
It dodges behind the bell-cote
and then appears as punched putty or a coin.
The key has a nail for the night
behind the snecked front door.
Carrying a tray of waters up to bed
I halt a careful tread to squint
through curtains not quite met
at the church, the moon, and the silver light
cast on the upturned breasts of the parish dead
locked out for the night.

The Surplice

To think so many battles have been fought
over this four and a half yard circumference
of white linen. Not just by those who ironed it
up to the difficult tucks beneath the yoke
but by Divines wrangling over rubrics.
For me it is my only finery, by law
decent and comely; a vestry friend
put on often in dread; given away
to old deft fingers to mend.
I have seen them hanging in as many ways
as there have been voices chanting in them:
immaculate in hanging wardrobes; or worn
with the peg mark still obtruding;
or chucked on the back seat of the car
with the purple stole and the shopping.
We have put these garments on for centuries.
They persist. We wither and crease inside them.

Churchyard under Snow

The newer headstones tense against the cold
having no moss to befriend the snow;
and footsteps to them are specific, directed
not for idle search, but to a particular bolster of earth.
Year long widowers right a tipped vase
and shake the Christmas wreath back into greenness.
A thrush cascades snow off a bouncing
high branch and offers its clear song
over the uniform white ground.
The cold makes it so much worse,
indiscriminate in its disregard
for the memory of this one's summer dress
and the angle of that one's cap over his shrewd brow.
We used to hurry them inside from the cutting wind:
now, from that unimaginable weathering
we can only trust their souls do well to fly.

Playing for England
(for Robert Hanvey)

He sat by the boot shop window
fettling the studs for Saturday's match,
his apron slashed almost to shreds.
As farm carts bounced back from the fields
he thought of the new schoolteacher,
and the match. The Match.
It kept coming back to that.

The lasts, the knife, and the needle
were set aside for the weekend
so he could scrummage with unaccustomed
other shoulders. He left the last shoe
to be mended, with the thread dangling.

Chosen to play for England
in the year of the General Strike
he shook the hand of George V
at Twickenham. His white strip engaging
the king's black overcoat and bowler.

Rose on the chest, buttons and collar;
full, pocketed shorts; bandage garters;
dubbin and embrocation.
The rest was himself:
solid, neckless Cumberland.

The match was the usual mixture
of dread and exultation, cracking of heads,
snotting out of one nostril.
He gum-shielded his half-time orange
and on his hunkers took in the tactics.
The scrum steamed as the light dwindled.

Feeding out the notched leather strap
for letting the window down of the last train
he was the only one to alight:
tasselled, velvet cap in the bag.

London was a single bird's song away.

They lost, but never mind.
There was the home ground
looking up to the mountains;
the schoolteacher encouraging
her African violets; and round about
the folks' shoes to make and mend.

Skiddaw House

The House was one of the loneliest dwelling-
places in all the British Isles
HUGH WALPOLE

Left for us to assume what purpose
it once had other than shelter;
remote in the bowl of hills behind Skiddaw
deep in its own decay; the peace stuns,
the filth accumulates, the questions gnaw.
How did anyone manage? Did they feed
on the shifting view of mountain tops?
Why put the windows facing north-east?
Some say it was for the shoot,
for nights away from the Big House
to be near the butts. Others that
it was given to shepherds
for weeks at a time, and they survived
because they knew there was somewhere else
nearer the auction and the ale.
Yet what if once it had been a family
living there, taking silver water from the beck
and setting off for a day's walk
to Keswick or Bassenthwaite.
Growing up taught by the hills' silence;
reading the shifting mist; working out God's pattern
from this piece of it. The larch coppice
smoothed into shape by the wind.
The gate into the four rows of vegetables
now on one hinge.

The Church Boiler

Robert W. Pitt Ltd. Milburn House (B Floor), Newcastle-on-Tyne.
For one new six Section Water Circulating Boiler supplied
and fitted in position to your satisfaction. Removing
old Boiler and connecting up to your existing pipes as
arranged – £41-10
             26th November, 1932

1st August, 1932

Dear Mr Pitt, I'm told
it's possible you have a better system
of heating to offer to a poor parish
than the old one we have, which is furred up
and has poor circulation, so that some radiators
are starved of heat. The complaints
are justified. Something must be done,
of course it must, and it is my
responsibility: not only preaching sermons
but also keeping the people warm.

10th September, 1932

I'm so pleased that you can help. Newcastle
seems a long way from Cumberland:
you and your man will spend the night, I hope,
and over here we have a man who helps.
We are so dependent on the goodwill
of the sexton. He does his best:
coming every Saturday night with his torch,
he shovels the coke, lights the boiler,
and carts away the ash. I can hear it
from the Vicarage but leave him to it
hoping he keeps a straight path to the ash-pit.
He will do anything for you except come to church.

15th September, 1932

You say the new boiler will be larger
and displace the coke. That will mean a new
coke pile and a lean-to for it. More work for the sexton;
more requests for kindness. How difficult I find that!
Bob will do it, but his pace
will signify that it's a favour. I'd do it myself
but then he'd say it was his job.

12th October, 1932

I don't understand the significance
of an increase of 20,000 Thermal Units.
All I know is what a difference it makes
to be warm, and how it will cost
more than we can think of or can easily manage to pay.
But this must be the story everywhere,
and a Sale will go a long way to meet the cost.
So whenever you and your man can come
we shall be pleased to see you. I'll ask the sexton
if he can help, when he's not busy at the Garage.

7th November, 1932

When you left last Monday
and we thought everything was fine
one of the small pipes on the boiler
had commenced to leak. There's always
something, isn't there. Could you get a new fitting
sent through with your man?
We would like to light up the boiler for the service
on the Twenty Third Sunday after Trinity.
For the last few Sundays
it's been cold here, but not severe.
How dependent we are in our Church for warmth.
We cater largely for the old.

23rd November, 1932

I'm sorry to trouble you again
but the boiler now seems to be overheating.
I know you'll understand if I say that a service
held under threat of an explosion is not conducive
to the rest and quietness advocated by the Evening Collect.
It makes everyone nervous. The sexton
says that it's probably easy to control
but he would value your opinion.

13th December, 1932

We have taken note of your suggestion
and installed, at least the sexton has,
a pipe which can take the overflow of boiling water.
That is a relief. Such a simple thing
needing just 'a little common reason' as you say.
We have put a thermometer by the lectern
so every time I read the lesson I think
of your common reason and the fount
of heavenly wisdom. The Sale helped raise the funds,
and we have pleasure in settling your account.

Hopkins Enters the Roman Catholic Church

Dressed mainly in black and with hair
shading the upper lip,
he took the railway from Oxford
to Birmingham; fingernails, collar, note book
all much grubbier than we would suppose.
The journey was an absolute offering
in the dark. The tunnels confirmed this.
The shattering thunder of iron
recalled the opposition to his choice:
Father, Mother, Canon Liddon –
'Do have the courage to stop, even now.'

In his note-book, the design
for a decanter stopper. Looking at the oaks
in the park he wondered how he would get
to the Oratory on the Hagley Road.
For comfort he thought that being alone
might double charge his spirit, but good,
they were expecting him, and yes,
he was Mr Hopkins and this was
all he had brought. They arrived in the dark,
and the leaves blown into the hall of the house
scratched on the chequered floor
as far as Doctor Newman's room.

For Norman Nicholson

It was a long way round from
Ulverston on the road to Millom.
We passed the low sands and the gulls
and the first outcrop of the hills
until at 'the west of the west'
– his phrase – we reached a film set
of the 1930s, stage and props.
You could tread on a whole row of shops
and chapels. So many corners to lean against.
So much shoring up of the corrugated fence.
That must be the house
with its old shop window doused,
where you can sit in the back
and join in the front street crack.
Over the roofs, Black Combe,
and yonder the silent doom
of Windscale. All this has been set
down in words, from the Good Friday sonnet
of the first wartime anthology
to the dazzle of the Easter Sunday sea.

David Wright

DAVID WRIGHT was born in Johannesburg, South Africa in 1920, and educated at Northampton School for the Deaf. At Oxford he was a contemporary of Sidney Keyes and John Heath-Stubbs. He has had a distinguished career as poet, editor, anthologist, and now divides his time between Cumbria and Portugal. His many books include *To the Gods the Shades* (Carcanet, 1976), *Metrical Observations* (Carcanet, 1980), *A View of the North* (MidNAG, 1976), and *Deafness: a personal account* (Allen Lane, 1969; Faber, 1990). His translation of Chaucer's *Canterbury Tales* into modern English appeared from OUP in 1985. ●

ACKNOWLEDGEMENTS: Carcanet Press and Greville Press; *Poetry Durham, Scotsman, Spectator.*

The Lakes

How probable to the eye, this collation
Of miniature wilderness, delicious lakes,
Where low-slung clouds lift eminences higher,
Hiding the apexes with vaporous flanks.

Aspects of water – cataract, stream and cloud,
Lake, mist, and river, modulate with stone
In all its forms – rock, boulder, scree, and crag –
To entertain and serve imagination.

Light converses between the fixed and shifting:
Cloudraker hills, the streams that lance and fade;
Each valley aerial in a vague refraction
Imposed upon the bosom of its lake.

Beyond them and behind, there where unbothered
Still pools look skyward, each a single eye,
Solitude like a wildflower to be gathered
Waits for the cursory footstep patiently.

How understandable to have apprehended
Nature and the God of nature on our side.
A valley counterpoints a mountain cadence;
A lovely sheet of water lies quiet;

And washed in evening, when light is clearest,
The panorama, thoroughly admired,
Glances at its reflection in the water
Like a young girl successfully attired.

Cockermouth

Past castle, brewery, over a sandstone bridge,
A Midland Bank, 'Fletcher's Fearless Clothing',
And huge effigy of an assassinated politician,
You come upon a Georgian grand frontage,

Still the town's 'big house', built for a Sheriff,
Not long ago ransomed from demolition
(The site an ideal one for the new bus-station)
And looked at, now, by a small bust of Wordsworth.

Turn down its by-lane leading to the river,
You'll see, fenced like a P.O.W. camp, reached by
An iron footbridge, the town's factory;
There ran a millrace, where was once a meadow,

And Derwent shuffles by it, over stones.
And if you look up the valley toward Isel
With Blindcrake to the north, cloudcatcher fells,
Whose waters track past here to Workington.

Eighteenth-century, like some town of Portugal;
Doorways faced with stone, proportionate windows,
And painted black and white, or gayer colours;
A scale perfectly kept, appropriately small.

Born here or hereabouts then: John Dalton,
Propounder of atomic theory; Fletcher
Christian; and, juxtaposing that Bounty mutineer,
Wordsworth the poet, of all unlikely men.

Tombs of shipmasters on the hill overlook
Town roofs, the valley where the river slips away
Toward the dead ports and the Irish sea,
Dowsed furnaces, closed mines of haematite

And coal, fortunes of Lowther and Curwen,
Slagheaps, the mansions of industrialists
Shuttered and rotting, burned or derelict,
Where a prosperity of impoverishment

Flourished, and now stands memorial
There, and in small classic facades of this town,
To the era designated Augustan;
Brown leaves about the baroque headstones fall.

On one side foundries; and the other way
Those frugal, delectable mountains
Where the smallholder yeoman, an anachronism,
Hung on into the nineteenth century.

So set, equidistant between past and future,
What more likely than, just here and then,
Should have been born that Janus-headed man,
A conservator and innovator

As the machine began to gather power,
Menacing nature to smile, because subdued?
The walled garden of his childhood
Stands as it was, pondering the river.

Caleb Barnes

Set on rising ground above the village
Is a memorial seat inscribed 'Caleb
Barnes', with a date, four years before my time,
'Twenty-six years the village schoolmaster'.
It looks toward a lake and famous mountains,
Skiddaw and Blencathra and Helvellyn,
And yet the focus of its contemplation
Turns from them, fixes on a bog between
Bassenthwaite and invisible Derwentwater:
A dingy morass, dyke-divided, whose
Dead paths and secret bridges Caleb Barnes
Only knew, and which now only I know,
Or so I think, because no one goes there:
Nothing to see but reedgrass; a mangrove
Copse of birdcherry, hornbeam, sunk in moss;
A few drowned fences of oxidized wire.
Because we loved the same neglected place
I feel I know the man I never met,
Although what drew him does not much draw me
Except as an occasional spectacle:
Orchids and water plants and waterfowl,
And, nameless to me, migrant winter birds.
All these he could, and did, identify,
A collector of life, of knowledge too;
Here he was happy and outside himself.
This is all I know about the man, except
The nondescript and untraversable flats
In different lights of winter, summer, spring,
And autumn, that shift round a bowl of hills
In clear or muffled weather; the altering
Colours of these four seasons that they wear;
I may suppose they meant as much to him.

Winter at Gurnard's Head

All a January day, in the house above the cliff,
From its window overlooking Gurnard's Head,
                                                      a coastguard hut,
The rocky bite of a cove, a lapsed harbour of cut stone,
Far and sheer the sea below, I sit in my chair alone

And watch through the pelt and drench of furious and spent spray
Lolloping down a pane – flung wet parings of the gale –

An iron cargo-boat, ears laid back, butting for sea-room
There between a steamgrey sky and its colouring cauldron.

What else or better to do, onlooker, than admire
The combat of air and water? – Unable to wish
Either to win, I only want neither to lose:
That sum of iron devices, and what's called nature.

**TO THE GODS THE SHADES
FLAVINUS OF THE CAVALRY
REGIMENT OF PETRIANA
STANDARD BEARER OF THE
WHITE TROOP AGED XXV
AND OF VII YEARS SERVICE
IS HERE BURIED**
(to Tony Harrison)

A rider in stone
Horse rearing high
As helmed and armed he
Spurns the bare bum
Bowed barbarian
Hovers a victory

But not to live long
Flavinus
To the Gods the Shades
And the naked man

With sword crouching
Whose death's to read

Written on stone
Horse and Roman
Standardbearer or
The hamstringer
Bent under to aim
Bare blade at them

The Musician

In the south aisle of the abbey at Hexham
I turned to make a remark on its Roman
Tomb; but she did not hear me, for the organ
Was playing in the loft above the rood-screen,
Laying down tones of bronze and gold, a burden
Of praise-notes, fingerings of a musician
There at the keys, a boy, his master by him,
Whose invisible sound absorbed my saying.

Music inaudible to me, barbarian,
But legible. I read in my companion
Its elation written in her elation.
'He is so young he can be only learning,
You would not have expected to hear such playing,
It's like a return to civilisation.'
Unable to hear, able to imagine
Chords pondering decline, and then upwelling

There in that deliberate enclave of stone,
I remembered music was its tradition;
Its builder, Acca, taught by one Maban
To sing; who may have been the god of song,
Mabon the god of music and the young;
That another bishop of this church, St John,
Taught here a dumb man speech, says Bede: became
Patron and intercessor of deaf men.

Juxtapositions

Six decades gone and one to come,
In summer leaves I read, autumn.

July foliage, winter form:
Beech in leaf and barebones elm.

I saw a salmon leap and fail,
Fail and leap where water fell.

A wake of wild geese flying by
A river mirroring their sky.

Low river, slow river, heron
Slow also, loth to go, going.

Those Walks We Took

Those walks we took I shall not take
Again. The meadows sloping to
A wooded, sunken, mud-brown beck
Where, brilliant, a kingfisher flew
A flash beneath the wooden bridge,
I shall not see: but recollect,
And so preserve a living Now
In which my loss may figure like
The autumnal and failing light
That washed the fields with dying gold.

Often we walked along that beck
And crossed its rotting bridge to find
A white farmhouse below the falls
Sometimes Niagara, sometimes
A straggle like a gap-toothed comb:
And where its water dug a pool
Were Christmas geese, and water-fowl,
Making a picture for the mind
To keep – no, not for ever, but
As long as one of us had breath.